Toronto Reprint Library of Canadian Prose and Poetry

Douglas Lochhead, General Editor

This series is intended to provide for
libraries a varied selection of titles of
Canadian prose and poetry which
have been long out-of-print. Each
work is a reprint of a reliable edition,
is in a contemporary library binding,
and is appropriate for public circula-
tion. The Toronto Reprint Library
makes available lesser known works
of popular writers and, in some cases,
the only works of little known poets
and prose writers. All form part of
Canada's literary history; all help to
provide a better knowledge of our
cultural and social past.

The Toronto Reprint Library is pro-
duced in short-run editions made
possible by special techniques, some
of which have been developed for
the series by the University of Toronto
Press.

This series should not be confused
with Literature of Canada: Poetry
and Prose in Reprint, also under the
general editorship of Douglas Lochhead.

UNIVERSITY OF TORONTO PRESS

Toronto Reprint Library of Canadian Prose and Poetry
©University of Toronto Press 1973
Toronto and Buffalo
Reprinted in paperback 2017
ISBN 978-0-8020-7513-0 (cloth)
ISBN 978-1-4875-9233-2 (paper)

Only publication was in 1859,
but in two versions. Entire poem
handset and printed by William Kirby
at the 'Mail' printing shop.
This reprint is the second version
of the poem, Kirby having made some
minor corrections and changes.

THE

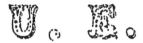

U. E.

A TALE OF

"Contented Toil, and hospitable Care,
And kind connubial Tenderness are there,
And Piety with wishes placed above,
And steady Loyalty and faithful Love."

NIAGARA. 1859.

PREFACE.

The following poem was written in the year 1846, and with much diffidence, is now, for the first time, published by its author. Its design was mainly to preserve a few peculiar traits of a generation of men, now alas! nearly passed away: the United Empire Loyalists of Canada; those brave and devoted defenders of the British Crown, Connexion and Government, in the American Revolution, that ended in the partition of the Empire, and the settlement of Upper Canada, by the Loyalist Refugees on the one hand, and the formation of the United States on the other. The author is conscious of many faults in his work; and although it has lain by, a longer time than Horace recommends even, he fears its quality will not have improved by the keeping, as it has been wholly neglected during that time. Such as it is however, he ventures to publish it, in the hope that his humble tribute to the memory of the noble Patriarchs of Upper Canada, who, with this goodly land, the fruit of their early toils and almost incredible hardships, have left us the still nobler inheritance of their patriotic and loyal example, may not be unacceptable to Canadian readers. For such must ever cherish the memory of the U. E. Loyalists, as a class of men who individually and almost without exception, deserved that fine encomium of the Roman poet.

" *Cui Pudor, et Justitiæ Soror,*
Incarrupta Fides, nudaque Veritas ;
Quando ullum invenient parem ?"

NIAGARA. 1859.

TO THE HON.

SIR JOHN BEVERLEY ROBINSON,

BARONET;

CHIEF JUSTICE OF UPPER CANADA.

THIS POEM IS (BY PERMISSION,)

RESPECTFULLY DEDICATED.

THAT HE MAY LONG CONTINUE, AS HE HAS LONG BEEN,

THE PRIDE AND ORNAMENT OF OUR LAND,

WHICH HE HAS IN TURN DEFENDED WITH HIS SWORD,

ILLUSTRATED WITH HIS ELOQUENCE

AND DISTINGUISH'D BY HIS SUPREME ADMINISTRATION

OF JUSTICE,

IS THE SINCERE DESIRE OF HIS MUCH OBLIGED

AND MOST OBEDIENT SERVANT,

THE AUTHOR.

THE U. E.

A TALE OF

UPPER CANADA.

Introduction.

In lone Canadian woods I raise my song,
Where lingering suns, the summer days prolong,
And rugged oaks, their lengthening shadows fling,
Athwart the sunshine of the silent spring,
While blue Ontario, sparkling through the trees,
With grateful breezes fans the hour of ease.

Let others far for foreign grandeurs roam,
Dearer to me the loveliness of home :
Our ocean-lakes that spread to regions strange,
Where beavers dam, and herding bisons range;
Our boundless woods where rapid rivers sweep,
And cloudy Cataracts in thunder leap,
Our hills and vales with verdure rich and rare,
'Neath azure skies that breathe immortal air,
Our bushy banks with birds and berries gay,
Our gentle streams that wind themselves away
Through flowery meads and fields of golden corn.
Where Plenty fills brimful her copious horn,
And cheerful toils and rural sports endear
Each varied season of the circling year.
But glorious Maro ! unto thee belong
The might and majesty of epic song.

And thine with power and grandeur to rehearse
In all the pomp of pan-harmonic verse,
Gods and their works, and on the Lyre unbar
The mighty symphonies of man and war.
Thee, Chief of song! Let circling halos blaze
Around thy head and crown immortal bays,
For me a wreath of modest cedar, still,
May haply bloom on some Canadian hill.
Then come my woodland Muse and fire my tongue,
And let my lips the moving strain prolong,
Till warm with life and radiant from above,
My lay be worthy of my country's love!

Canto First.

I.

And first what lit my soul and poet's pride,
Yon Mansion seated on the upland side,
Where shady orchards lovingly surround,
And glistening vanes o'ertop the rising ground;
Where winding through the forest glades, are seen,
Meadows and cornfields, all in gorgeous green,
And flocks and herds, in grassy pastures run,
Or in the reedy pool defy the noonday sun.
Could my unpracticed hand, with truth portray,
And virtue in a fitting guise array,
Imperial Cæsar, in his proudest hour,
Might vail his grandeur at yon simple door.

II.

Ah! thou sweet bard, who sawest with mournful eye
"The rural virtues from their Country fly,"
Here mightst behold them in their new-found home,
The inmates of this hospitable dome.

Hearts, there together knit in fondest ties;
With innocence and love supremely wise,
In cheerful labours pass their peaceful days,
While grateful evening all their toil repays.
Unseen, unenvied, in that blissful bower,
The gauds of fashion or the pomps of power ;
And Schoolmen there, the use of life might scan,
And learn that serving God is love to man.

III.

Now down in yonder mead where clover grows,
Fragrant, as honey sweet, and ruddy glows,
A sun-burnt band all lithe and bending sway,
With sinewy arms, the scythe, and toss the hay.
A shaggy house-dog, and a lovely boy,
His widowed mother's solace, pride and joy,
With noisy glee, and merry riot, play
Half-buried rolling in the new mown hay.
And sitting in the shade of yonder trees,
To view their labours and recline at ease,
The aged sire of him, who scythe in hand,
With rural triumph heads the rustic band.
The old man smiles with happy look benign,
And in his son still leads the harvest line.
His flowing locks of venerable grey,
Adorn a brow clear as the sunny day,
Thoughtful and kind, though traced with many a care,
No meanness ever set a wrinkle there.
His placid lip, his mild composed eye,
Beaming with light of an immortal sky,
His stalwarth frame, and upright bearing, scan,
On every single part is stamped, the man.

IV.

But where's Constance, who from his side hath gone,
The widow of his first-born favorite son,

Who yonder lies where weeping willows wave
And mournful bend above his humble grave?
His gallant Ethwald, who, when wild alarms,
Rang through the land, Rebellion was in arms!
Forsook his fields and seized his rifle true,
And bade his dear Constance a last adieu;
His noble heart on fire, he rushed with speed,
To save his country at her utmost need;
And still pressed foremost of the faithful band,
Who quelled invasion and preserved the land:
Until, from Prescott's plain, where cold he lay,
His weeping father bore his corse away.

V.

But where is Constance? lo! she's gone to lave,
With tears, the flowers that deck her hero's grave.
And by the grassy hillock, kneeling low,
Pours out her bosom's agonizing woe;
While severed memory rushing through the brain,
Brings up the past, and Ethwald lives again,
As when he crossed the seas in hope and pride,
To make his boyhood's love, his manhood's bride
Ah! happy day at last! no more to part,
She clasped her faithful lover to her heart,
While little reck'd she that his manly bloom,
So soon would wither in the silent tomb.

VI.

The father sees with sympathizing woe,
His favorite lie convulsed in passion's throe,
With throbbing heart, and filled with dire alarms,
He flies and lifts her in his trembling arms.
Unconscious droops her head—a pallid flower,
Whose stem is broken by the tempest's power.
Her auburn locks' rich foldings all untressed,

Their golden flood pour o'er his pitying breast,
While with affection's tenderness he fanned
Her snowy cheek, and with his hollow hand
Drew crystal drops from out the gushing sp.ing,
And fondly watched life's feeble fluttering wing.
Young Eric, who but now was singing blythe,
As low he bent and swung his sweeping scythe,
Perceives his father run, nor sooner views
Than like a bounding deer, at once pursues.

VII.

The labourers all alarmed, leave off their song,
Forsake their work and round their mistress throng,
Their rugged bosoms melt with sympathy,
For as a mother, kind to all was she.
But where's her boy, her rosy blue-eyed boy,
The image of his Sire, her only joy?
Ah! round her neck he twines his tiny arms,
With tears and kisses her cold cheek he warms,
While, at her feet the shaggy Hector lies,
Imploring looks and whines with piteous cries.
Her child's soul-piercing tones, how deep they dart
In the unconscious mother's inmost heart!
Wake her from death, as once the Orphean strain,
Drew lost Eurydice to life again.
Their cares revive, and as she clasped her child,
For thee alone I live! she cried in accents wild.

VIII.

O! Woman's heart! what tongue can ere explain,
Th' expanse of love thy narrow walls contain,
The ceaseless working which thy depths reveal
When some loved hand takes off the covering seal?
The blooming maid, so light in pleasure's hour,
Her only thought to wield her beauty's power,
Array her locks, alternate frown and smile,

With airy fancies changing all the while.
See that fair girl, a wife and mother now,
The crown of love sits on her duteous brow;
Still more sublime, when dark misfortunes lour,
When Want assails, and Death knocks at the door,
When grim, with poisonous breath, he stikes his prey,
And from her arms her loved ones tears away;
O! then the depth of woman's love explore,
And its infinity, like heaven's, adore.

IX.

Constance! such love was thine, and worthy him,
Whose cup of bliss thou filledst to the brim.
Well I recall the day, in Autumn hale,
When through these forests ran the happy tale,
" Young Ethwald is returned, and by his side,
Leads to his father's home a blooming bride."
His sire beloved by all who worth adore,
Blest be the hour that brought him to our shore;
Long years are past since first these spreading trees,
Sheltered the wanderer from the cool night breeze,
And times and times, the leaves their prime renewed,
Ere he the forest wilderness subdued;
But now, abundant wealth rewards his pains,
Primeval woods are turned to fruitful plains,
His generous heart no longer checks its glow,
Nor longs to give with nothing to bestow.

X.

Upon the grassy banks of winding Swale,
Their ancient homestead graced the pleasant dale,
Its walls with honeysuckles over-run,
Its lattice windows shining in the sun,
Its tiled roof with gables pointing o'er
The carved lintels, and inviting door
With well-worn threshold, marked the rural dome,

Of yore, old Walwyn's and his fathers' home,
A sturdy Oak that braved the tempest's jars,
Since mighty Edward led his northern wars,
Outstretched its giant arms wide o'er the green,
And cooled the summer day with shade serene.
All Walwyn's sires had played their infant plays,
Beneath its boughs and soothed life's closing days. ;
With that brave tree, full long they bore the blast,
With it, decay sapped down their strength at last.
The fields around, enclosed with hedges neat,
Where shady nooks and bubbling runnels meet,
Were still the same, this sober race had trod
And tilled, and reaped, and grateful thanked their God.
With all the needy tribe for miles around,
Their hospitable name was foremost found,
While those who nicer scanned, were sure to tell
Sense, honesty and worth were theirs as well.

XI.

But England, then began to taste of woes,
Her halcyon days drew fast towards a close,
When Walwyn erst succeeded to his Sire
And faithful labored with unflagging fire,
Till middle age came on, when dark o'erspread,
Misfortune's clouds swept round his manly head;
For woe the day! the partner of his breast
Left him in two fair boys, her last bequest.
In vain he toiled, and every art applied,
His farm no more increasing wants supplied,
The wealth laid by in happier days before,
Grew daily less and dwindled more and more.
With Summer's droughts, and Autumn's drenching
        rains,
His blackened crops lay sweltering on the plains,
Contagion seized his flocks, and one by one
His murrained herd expired with piteous moan,
While taxes scarce in plenteous years sustained,

Swept from his fields the little that remained.

XII.

The greatest this of all old England's woes,
Her children's grief and joyaunce of her foes,
Sad price for freedom saved, yet needful paid,
When half the world to Gaul submission made,
And ravaged Europe torn and mangled lay
Th' Imperial soldier's vile dishonored prey.
England alone, behind whose bulwarks ran
The vestal virtues, and the hopes of man,
From first to last, maintained the holy cause
Of justice, liberty and social laws.
Through years accursed to strife she fought and bled,
Her best and bravest numbered with the dead,
Spent her estate, and risked her very name,
To save the world from tyranny and shame.
And when th' Imperial captive borne in chains
Left peace at length on Europe's trampled plains,
It came unblessing ; for succeeding years
From war entailed the nation's deep arrears,
And want and suffering scourged th' exhausted land
Till peace seemed worse than war and harder to with-
  stand.

XIII.

All this knew Walwyn well, for of his heart
His country ever shared the greater part,
And while he mourned her fate and felt the curse
Saw factions rage who had still turned to worse,
With infamy, each generous motive brand,
Their King revile and curse their native land,
He sadly turned him to the Western breeze,
And thought of regions far beyond the seas,
Where freedom, peace and plenty all combine,
And still rejoice 'neath England's rule benign.

Alas! he murmured, and if. I must roam,
Be there my country, and be there my home!

XIV.

He thought of all his past domestic joys,
His clouded hopes, and then his rising boys,
Mid others plenty seen reduced to want,
To beg a crust, and hear the bitter taunt,
Or clad in misery craving leave to toil,
And with their sweat and tears bedew the soil,
While some harsh master grudgingly may spread
The scanty pittance of their daily bread.
The thought envenomed, like an adder stung,
And drops of anguish on his forehead hung.
Great God! he cried, and shall I live to see
Their blooming cheeks worn thin by penury,
The tasted cup of knowledge dashed aside,
And shrivelled Want. each nobler aim divide?
No! no! he cried, I'll take my staff in hand,
And guide their footsteps to the Western strand,
For their dear sakes I'll leave my native shore,
Never, alas! to see my country more!

XV.

Ah! painful choice, can nothing change the doom,
Plenty abroad, or penury at home?
No! he must flee ere ruin's final birth,
And poverty has quenched his friendly hearth;
Must leave at last the green hills of his sires,
Where first his heart beat strong with youthful fires,
The hallowed grove where on his faithful breast,
His Hilda's lips the mutual flame confessed,
The neighbouring cots, the distant rising moor,
The pebbly stream with willows shaded o'er,
The hedge-row lane that forty years he trod,
To pay his Sabbath homage to his God.

XVI.

The bitter day is come—their partings o'er
With breaking hearts they leave their native shore,
The fading coast sinks fast beneath their eyes,
And one blue watery circle bounds the skies;
The Pilot calls his boat, and from the side
With him, the last fond links of home divide.
But mark that youth absorbed in silent grief,
The changing scene to him brings no relief.
Though scarce sixteen, these are no childish tears,
That weep some toy despised in riper years.
The last dim speck of land arrests his eyes,
And sinks, and still he looks and still he sighs,
While memory conjuring up each parted scene,
Turns watery wastes to groves and meadows green:
Again he roves along the banks of Swale
And tunes his pipe adown the bleating vale;
Again, with lovely Constance by his side,
Sweet words and kinder looks his care divide;
In childhood linked, they wont the fields to rove,
In riper youth, instinctive sought the grove,
Till to their throbbing hearts an utterance came,
They knew they loved, and passion found a name.

XVII.

First love, thou dawn of heaven! let none despise,
But know thy holy flame comes from the skies.
Repelled from manhood's selfish scheming breast,
In youth's pure heart, it finds congenial rest,
With tender empire, every feeling sways,
And gilds all future life with Orient rays.
The world may warp, and disappointment chill,
But to its earliest passion faithful still,
The treasured vows of youth, the heart will hold,
More precious than the miser keeps his gold.

XVIII.

Bright rose the sun on that unhappy morn
These youthful lovers were asunder torn,
Who like two saplings grown each other round,
Rudely untwisted, droop unto the ground.
That morn, the lark trilled sweet the song of day
To cheer his spouse that in the long grass lay;
The blooming hawthorns all their fragrance yield
And sportive lambs skip o'er the daisied field;
But nature wore to them a dismal pall,
The merry tongues of morn unheeded call,
And long in other's arms they speechless stayed,
Till low, with courage feigned, young Ethwald said.

XIX.

Sweet Constance! Hope and day-spring of my life,
My boyhood's pride, and manhood's promised wife,
Thine anguished looks compel my wretched heart
To seek the comfort, it would fain impart.
Deem not ambition tempts my feet to rove,
To leave my country and forsake my love;
Hard Fate ordains, and o'er the Western sea
I seek a better home for love and thee.
Then send me not away oppressed with fears,
That thou may weep, and I not dry thy tears;
Think for a while thy Ethwald must depart
Again to come and clasp thee to his heart;
That heart where mirrored on its surface clear
Where ere I go, whatever fate I bear,
Stamped by the rays of love with art divine,
Thy beauteous image shall eternal shine.

XX.

To which the Maid with trembling voice, replied:
Forgive my heart, alas! too sorely tried,

The words thou speakest ever seem the best,
But thy dear words no longer calm my breast.
Weep not, sayst thou ? alas! from eve to morn,
From morn to eve, I'll weep till thou return ;..
For what can comfort, when a raging sea,
And half a world divide my love and me?
This grove, this spot, we used to call so fair,
That heard our vows shall hear my daily prayer
For thee restored, and on this mossy stone,
I'll count the weary moments one by one.
My Ethwald! thou wast ever tender, true,
And thought apart from thee, I never knew ;
Thy vows and holy promises shall rest
Like precious jewels treasured in my breast;
Come life ! come death ! whatever land or sea
May bring to pass, I love alone but thee !

XXI.

She stopped and on his bosom drooped her head,
'Twas but a passing cloud, that instant fled ;
His soul gazed on her from his azure eyes,
And in their depths she saw true hope arise.
'Tis past, she said; let not my Ethwald fear
Constance may be too weak her fate to bear.
Yes ! as the sun descended only seems
Awhile retired to rise with brighter beams,
So ever faithful thou again wilt come
To bless thy love and lead her to thy home.
Now go! now go! my eyes with darkness fill—
I see thee not—O God! but hold thee still—
A moment stay!—he's gone, and like a dart,
Each parting footstep smote her breaking heart.

XXII.

But lapsing time doth dull the edge of grief,
The gentlest nurse that brings the heart relief,

And Hope beams mildly as the polar star
Through breaking clouds when tempests cease to war.
Young Ethwald's soul grew patient and serene,
Though gone the joyous mirth that once had been,
A chastened light diffused its mellow rays
Like Indian-Summer's soft and golden haze,
Composed his looks and filled his eyes with thought,
And all the boy at once to manhood brought.
With filial love his aged sire he tends,
Or through the ship his watchful eye defends
The heedless steps where little Eric strays,
And with the jovial crew, exulting plays.
The crew lie round in groups, with small avail
They pipe the loitering winds to fill the sail
That hangs in folds and idly flaps the mast;
While on the deep, as if embedded fast,
The ship sits motionless in proud disdain,
Like some huge rock that juts upon the plain.

XXIII.

A dreamy stillness hovers o'er the deep,
And weary thoughts compose themselves to sleep.
The cloudless skies look down, and face to face,
Impress old Ocean with a long embrace.
The flaming sun shoots down his startling beams,
To depths where Midgard's hoary serpent dreams
Of coming doomsday, as he restless glows,
While banished mermaids fan his scaly brows.
Upon the placid surface, dashing spray
Of silver, marks the Dolphin's rapid play,
And troops of flying-fish exulting spring,
Defiant of the sea-bird's swooping wing.
The grampus slowly turns his bulky side,
'Mid little nautili that round him glide,
Erect their purple sail and ply their oar
And cruise in fairy fleets the ocean o'er.

2

XXIV.

The broad expanded waters tremulous, seem
Crusted with light beneath the solar beam.
A shining path of molten gold, anon,
Bridges the ocean to the setting sun,
Where seven-fold glories fill the glowing West,
And Heaven reveals its gorgeous halls of rest.
There, gates of Pearl iridescent, unfold
The streets of God paved with transparent gold,
And Fancy hears the sweet commingled tone
Of Angels' harps, and voices round the throne.
A glorious shadow of the real and true !
Incomprehensible but to the few,
Whose purged vision see the cords of light
That earth to heaven, and heaven to earth, unite !

XXV.

Old Ocean now unwonted slumber takes ;
But mark the hour when fresh the giant wakes,
And chides the truant zephyrs' idle race,
Who ceased to fan his broad reclining face.
At last he stirs, and on the very edge
Of sea and sky, appears a darker ledge ;
A coming ripple heralds in the wind,
And bulky clouds come trailing on behind.
In thronging droves the Porpoise rolls along,
And lusty breezes pipe their rising song.
The sails swell out, the streamers play above,
And soon the stately ship begins to move.
So moves the graceful stag who snuffs the gale,
And smells the hunter following on the trail ;
With flanks in-drawn, and nostrils stretched wide
He stamps his hoof and peers on every side,
He hears the bay of his approaching foes,
And swiftly bounding through the woodland goes.

XXVI.

Now harder gusts scud o'er the thickening skies,

In ridges deep and long the waters rise.
Amid the shrouds, the winds begin to wail,
And dashing sprays bedew the tightened sail.
As lowering skies o'erspread with deeper brown,
The pitching ship toils heavier up and down ;
The rumbling din of storms is heard afar,
And all betokens elemental war.
The watchful sailors hear the approaching gales,
Take in their spars, and reef their bursting sails,
And clear their cumbered decks, and all prepare,
To meet the viewless demons of the air.

XXVII.

Young Ethwald viewed the scene ; unwonted fire
Gleamed in his eyes as came the tempest nigher,
Wild throbbed his heart and mingled awe and joy,
Thrilled every nerve of the enraptured boy.
So feels the soldier, yet in wars unsteeled,
When first preparing for the martial field ;
His soul to tension strung, joys, hopes and fears,
Mix in his breast, and tingle in his ears.
The coward quails, the gross heart never knows
The terror sweet, from scenes like these that flows ;
The God-like rising of the raptured soul,
'Mid crash of worlds and elements that roll.

XXVIII.

The aged Sire beheld the raging scene,
With Christian confidence and tranquil mien ;
While on his lap his little Eric lay,
Smiled in his sleep, and dreamed of his play.
Ethwald, said he ; 'Tis moments such as these,
That try the soul and prove its boasted ease.
'Tis not when sensual joys the bosom lull,
And sophistries the eye of reason dull,
That we discern, how far we've gone astray

From virtue's path, and truth's eternal way.
But when a scene like this o'ertakes the soul,
When sea and sky in one convulsion roll,
When life hangs doubtful in the trembling scale,
And fiery tongues arraign us through the gale,
Depute of God; ah! then, the wakened mind
Sees Death elate, careering on the wind;
Conscience with horror plumed, her slumbers fled,
In shrieking resurrection yields her dead;
Each hidden sin comes forth in Fury's form,
Flits through the gloom and grins amid the storm,
But blest the man, whose steps have faithful trod
The path of duty, humbly serving God,
He leans upon his rock nor fears the blast,
Tho' each impending moment seem the last.
Like some firm lighthouse 'mid the howling gale
All's calm within, though thousand storms assail.

XXIX.

Now hissing thunderbolts around them fly,
The bellowing thunder shakes the murky sky;
The foaming waves unloose their horrid hair
And mountains high, roll up the realms of air;
While mournful voices pipe the gusts between
Like spirits wailing o'er the furious scene.
The hardy steersmen to the helm are tied,
And the huge wheel revolves from side to side,
To poise the ship beneath the straining sail
That swoops terrific down the driving gale.
Now plunging deep and buried in the spray,
She sinks in watery gulfs, lost to the day;
Now from their gloomy throat upbelched, springs,
She soars aloft, as borne on mighty wings,
And from the stormy peaks in prospect wide
Sees watery Alps heave up on every side;
Waves rolled on waves, until the foaming heap
Bursts like a snow drift o'er the raging deep.

XXX.

The rushing ship still hurries madly on
Until the vortex of the storm is won,
When wheels the hurricane with counter blast
And drives the sails upon the reeling mast.
The ship unpoised turns broadside to the storm
And in the sea-trough rolls a helpless form,
That now her end submerging, now her side,
Each dreadful moment threatens to divide.
The stout commander to the bulwark springs,
Faint through the din, his startling trumpet rings :
Destruction's on the ship if courage fail,
And none run out to cut that fatal sail !
But Providence, which ne'er remits its care,
Oft works deliverance when we most despair,
And that by human means whene'er it can,
Pleased to depute its own sweet grace to man.

XXXI.

Defying death, a gallant sailor sprung,
And on the whirling spars he climbed and clung ;
His hair streamed in the wind, his sparkling eye
And compressed lips, declared his courage high ;
With lion's grasp upon the point he springs,
And draws his knife and cuts the tangled strings.
The sail set free, the yard with swift recoil,
Dips in the surges that beneath him boil,
The angry winds drive up the blinding spray,
A victim has been doomed, and this their prey,
His hands relax—another whirlwind raves,
And sweeps him headlong in the yawning waves,
A moment seen, he signs a last farewell,
And sinks forever 'neath the foaming swell.
The ship relieved, wears round with horrid jar,
Obeys her helm and stretches to the war,
Firm sets her head against the winds and tides,

And in its very teeth, the tempest rides.
So the brave man pursued by host of foes
Too hotly pressed, turns round and meets their blows,
To desperation strung, in urgent need
Finds greatest safety in the boldest deed.

XXXII.

At length the storm subsides, a gentler blast
And breaking clouds declare the tempest past;
The welcome sun peeps through its shattered screen,
And pours a yellow light o'er all the scene.
The wearied ocean sunk in gentler swells
Hides deep its victim in its briny cells,
Where corals inter-twine, and mosses wave,
And sea shells dirge around his watery grave.
Brave heart, said Ethwald, which at duty's call
Gave for our safety, its life, and all,
The clustering hopes of manhood's youthful prime
Like summer fruit that's shaken e'er its time.
What though unnoted in the roll of fame,
Thy honest lineage, and thy humble name,
But few of Glory's laurelled sons possessed
A nobler spirit or a warmer breast!
Not Curtius leaping in the dark abyss,
Rome's choicest sacrifice, outrivalled this,
Not St. Pierre, when he devoted wound
The shameful halter his brave neck around,
On him more glorious than the golden string,
That decked the breast of England's furious king,
When Calais opened her blockaded gate,
And bowed submissive to the hand of Fate.

XXXIII.

Poor nameless mariner! though never thine,
The civic crown and elegy divine,
Nor carved stone to claim a pitying sigh,

And tell thy story to each passer by ;
Else would thy just remembrance long endure,
And humane eyes lament, in drops as pure
As ever trickled from a mountain well,
Or sparkled in a rainbow as they fell.
Yet some may wait thy coming and with glee
Their humble cottage deck to welcome thee :
But who shall tell, what plastic words can show,
A mother's anguish or a lover's woe,
When back, the home-bound ship salutes the shore,
And thou be numbered with her crew no more ?
And what know I, but that tempestuous gale,
Raged through the willows on the banks of Swale,
Where haply Constance bowed her lovely form
And for our safety prayed amid the storm ?
Ah ! doubly ransomed if I live the care
Of generous daring and of beauty's prayer !
Let me be mindful that the precious seed
Of such example grow to equal deed,
And teach my soul in sunshine and in storm,
With life or death, my duty to perform.

XXXIV.

The father faintly smiled to hear his boy,
While starting drops his shaggy eye-lids cloy.
How 'twas I know not; but his look betrayed.
Some sudden thought o'ercast a moment's shade.
Right, Ethwald ! Right ! he said, in serious tone,
Our first great duty is to God alone ;
Our country next demands her sacred dues,
And ne'er may son of mine her claim refuse.
I cannot blame thee, if, some fatal day,
Like him, should see thee give thy life away
'Tis what I taught thee, what I still commend,'
Though heaven avert so rude, untimely end.
May honored age come on thee, free from strife,
Blest with the tenor of a well-spent life.

For who, his honest calling worthily fills,
Whom neither envy gnaws, nor avarice chills,
Who uses riches as a trust from heaven ;
And fears not poverty if that be given ;
Who loves his country and obeys her laws,
Honours his king and warms in Freedom's cause :
That man no less adorns his native land
Than he who for her draws the warrior's brand.

XXXV.

In converse meet thus spake the son and sire,
Mingling their souls and fanning virtue's fire ;
While round the decks in groups, their brethern stand,
In joyless sport, or weary sigh for land.
Long weeks have past since from their country borne
'Mid boundless seas ; uprooted and forlorn,
Unsettled, racked with doubts and gloomy cares,
They weep the native seats no longer theirs ;
And sadly ponder, what will be the scenes
For which they left their cots and village greens.
Sometimes with changed mood, Hope lights the gloom,
And fancy pictures forth some future home,
Fast by embowering woods, where, clear and still,
Through fields their own, glides soft some gentle rill.

XXXVI.

Thus to and fro, conflicting passions sway,
And hopes and fears, alternate rule the day ;
Thus through the rack of clouds, the labouring moon
A moment flushes, and withdraws as soon.
What generous heart but sympathizing swells,
When the poor Emigrant his story tells !
Of home bereft, beneath the Western sun,
He fondly hoped new rounds of bliss to run ;
To see once more his wife and children smile,
Sharing the just rewards of honest toil,

Let none despise ! but know, 'tis such as these,
That bear the seeds of Empire o'er the seas ;
In farthest lands, plant Britain's mighty name,
Spread her dominion, and exalt her fame !

Canto Second.

I.

The gallant ship speeds on with swelling sails,
The dog-vanes dancing in the merry gales ;
Her prow cuts deep, through showers of silvery spray,
And traces far behind, a feathery way.
At length she strikes the Gulf Stream's mighty flow
Of turbid waters, steaming as they go,
Still warm from tropic skies and palmy lands,
To cheer bleak Prima Vista's fishy sands.
While tangled moss and sea-weeds floating by,
Give signs at last that land is drawing nigh.

II.

Omen of hope ! such great Columbus blessed,
When first his keel the virgin waters pressed ;
And wondering breezes wafted o'er the main,
The fall of Incas and the fate of Spain.
His piercing eye with fire of genius fraught,
Foresaw new Indies clothe the daring thought
Long pondered in his soul ; and firm and fast
His life-long dream, incarnate Truth at last.
Those worthless lichens to his raptured sight
Than strings of Orient diamonds seemed more bright,
Presaging as they floated slowly by
The vast new world emerging to his eye.
Father of Emigrants ! too great, too good !

For those whose cruel lusts were gold and blood;
Great in thy glory! greater mid thy pains!
The world still weeps and wonders at the chains,
That formed thy sad reward and called down
Eternal shame on Castile's royal crown.

III.

Scarce less rejoiced than he, our seaworn band
Shrill from the mast-head, hear the cry of land!
Land! Land! rings round the ship, a cheering cry
And round th' horizon sweeps each eager eye.
A faint blue speck appears; the anxious crowd,
Some call it land; and some a rising cloud;
Till fixed and clear, no longer doubt remains,
And long blue coasts obstruct the watery plains.
Now steer they in the Gulf. With sullen roar
Pour down the chilly winds of Labrador,
Where on the ice the herding walrus plays,
And glossy seals bask in the slanting rays,
And Dwarfish Esquimaux, with caution steal,
Their oily prey, and dress their nauseous meal.

IV.

Speeds on the gallant ship. Her course she bends
Against the floods great Cataraqui sends,
To hail the flag, her lofty peak sustains,
Liege lord of all his waters, hills and plains,
And many a land beyond, where rivers run
To Arctic seas, or shines the Western sun,
Grey wreaths of mist on distant headlands lie;
Green fir-clad islets cheer the weary eye;
The land-birds flutter 'mong the snowy sails,
And rising smoke upon the horizon trails;
A token sure, in which, they pleased, descry,
Man and his labours to be drawing nigh.

V.

Now far behind them lies a noisome strand
Where low-browed rocks oppress the sea-washed sand,
And Gaspe's fishers draw with ample seine,
The scaly tribute of the bounteous main.
Now Tadousac appears, upon whose strand
Malo's bold mariner first strode to land,
And planted in the bleak, unnurtured soil
The Fleur de lys ; the Briton's future spoil.
Now passed deep Saguenay who draws his floods
From lakes that hide in dark and pathless woods,
That bend and crash beneath the flying moose,
When swift the snow-shoed Indian pursues,
Now passed the lofty cliffs, whose heavy brows,
Still streaked and flecked with Winter's lingering snows,
Rise high above the mist that sweeps their sides
And gaze serenely on the rushing tides.
Around their base the mew and eagle scream,
The waves dash high, and dancing in the gleam
Of streaks of sunshine, many a whitened sail
Careers rejoicing in the lusty gale.

VI.

At length they spy huge Tourment, sullen-browed,
Bathe his bald forehead in a passing cloud ;
The Titan of the lofty Capes that gleam
In long succession down the mighty stream.
When lo ! Orleans emerges to the sight,
And woods and meadows float in liquid light :
Rude nature doffs her savage mountain dress,
And all her sternness melts to loveliness.
On either hand stretch fields of richest green,
With glittering village spires and groves between;
And snow-white cots adorn the fertile plain,
Where grazing flocks or distant moving wain,
Or human figure, though but half descried,

Pour life upon the landscape far and wide.

VII..

Now passed the Island portal; opens free
A glorious bay, fair as a summer sea;
Where boats and birds expand their mingled wings,
And many a princely ship at anchor swings,
While the reclining shore's immense concave
Of fields and gardens, drinks the crystal wave,
And sweeps away, till round th' Horizon seen,
Enfolding hills, the beauteous vision screen.
Afar, Quebec exalts her crest on high,
Her rocks and battlements invade the sky;
The pride of Canada, her strength and head;
England's assurance and Columbia's dread.
Her rampired rock appears 'mid nature's charms,
Like Mars reposing in fair Venus' arms,
His ponderous spear with flowery garlands hung,
Peace in his eye and friendship on his tongue.

VIII.

Softly the king of day reclining, spreads
His mantle o'er the crisped stream, and sheds
His slantant rays, rich as the golden shower
That ushered Jove into the Argive Bower.
'Neath rows of trees the whitened houses stand,
The fisher's. boats lie basking on the strand;
The light calèche speeds o'er the dusty road,
And peasants trudge beneath their market load.
Ere long they see a cloud of vapour soar
Like a pale phantom on the midway shore;
The high projecting bank is rent in twain,
And a dark chasm yawns upon the plain,
Where deep within, o'er precipices thrown,
A white cascade rolls like a curtain down.
O'erhanging trees, half seen 'mid clouds of spray,

Spring from the rocks that wall the narrow way,
Their dark green foliage trembling on each bough,
With every gust that rises from below.
Deep in its rocky bed, the boiling mass
Of waters rushes through the narrow pass,
Flies to the bosom of the tranquil bay,
Where like a frightened child it sobs its fear away.
Like stately swan that scuds before the gale,
The ship glides on and slowly shortens sail.
The ponderous anchor falls, the sudden gun,
With glad salute, proclaims her journey done.
Now cheers of joy burst from the eager crowds,
That throng the decks or climb the lofty shrouds;
Than all they yet beheld or thought, I ween,
Their wondering eyes survey a grander scene.

IX.

O, glorious sight! as golden sunset showers
Athwart the long-drawn walls and lofty towers;
Corruscant rays play round the cross-topped spires
And gild each salient point with shimmering fires.
Half screened 'mid countless masts, an endless maze
Of quays and roofs spring from the watery haze;
While on the Bay's broad bosom, far and wide,
The anchored fleets of commerce proudly ride.
Huge cliffs above, precipitous that frown,
Like Atlas bend beneath another town,
Where all along the grey embrasured steep
In grim repose the watchful cannon peep,
Tall spires, and domes, and turrets shine afar
Behind the arched gates, and mounds of war,
While proud Cape Diamond towers above them all,
With aerial glacis and embattled wall;
Till on the loftiest point where birds scarce rise,
Old England's standard floats amid the skies.

X.

O ! glorious spot !   The Briton's boast and pride,
Where armies battled and where heroes died,
Where gallant Wolfe led his devoted band,
Rejoiced in death, and waved his dying hand ;
'Mid cheers of Victory rung from side to side,
The hero smiled content, and calmly died,
Though few his years and young his lofty fame,
With greenest garlands, England crowns his name,
And on her roll of glory, proudly reads
The eternal records of his mighty deeds.
And noble Montcalm ! well thy honoured bier,
May claim the tribute of a British tear.
Although the lillies from these ramparts fell,
Thy name, immortal with great Wolfe's shall dwell.
Like him, the consciousness of duty done,
Soothed thy last pang and cheered thy setting sun.

XI.

Now from the East, Morn's golden javelins fly,
And crimson streamers sweep the kindling sky ;
The morning gun salutes the orb of day,
And sweet the distant drums beat reveille.
The sluggish mist that hid the reeking stream,
Rolls off in clouds before the orient beam ;
While slender rising smokes and busy hums
Proclaim the waking town its toil resumes.
But how forlorn, look round the stranger band
From yonder ship, who group upon the strand !
The little household treasures that they bore,
Lie piled in heaps or strown upon the shore.
May few unmoved, behold that disarray ;
These relics thrown exposed to roofless day,
Which once adorned, with all a house-wife's pride
Some happy home and cheerful ingle-side.

XII.

Yon lusty seats perchance, have once been seen
Set in the shade upon the village green,
Where age reclined and quaffed the nut-brown ale,
O'er country news and many a marvellous tale,
Or in the dusky eve, their sports begun,
The blythsome youths forgot their labours done,
While pipe and tabor struck a sprightly sound,
And nimble feet tripped many a rustic round.
Yon chest, quaint carved with many an oaken flower,
Of some great grand-dame formed the stately dower,
Yon massive couch has nursed the sweet repose
From labour, peace and love, that only flows.
Heir-loom, with every holiest thought combined,
That thrills the heart to memory resigned!
The nuptial throng oft led the blooming bride,
Whose sire and son sequent, were born and died.

XIII.

And when to other lands, stern fate decreed.
The mournful Sire his little ones should lead,
These precious fragments of his ancient dome,
He fondly hoped would cheer some future home.
So Æneas, when he bore his aged sire,
Through crumbling streets and blood, and raging fire,
And saved 'mid countless toils, his darling boy
To found in other climes a happier Troy;
The light of home, his household gods he bore,
T' assuage his grief and cheer some foreign shore;
Haply their presence, in his darker hours,
Might wile his soul to Ida's untorn bowers,
And let sad memory awhile repose
From thoughts of Troy's unutterable woes.

XIV.

As morn advances, warming by degrees,

A busy crowd swarms o'er the spacious quays,
The noisy ships disgorge their varied stores,
And piled cargos cumber all the shores ;
While bands of labourers toiling in the sun
Undam the stream of wealth and roll it on.
With sharp observant look, Old Walwyn's eye
Surveys the varied groups that pass him by :
Merchants intent on multiplying gains ;
And jovial sailors fresh from watery plains ;
And hardy raftsmen from the upper floods
Who float the mighty harvest of the woods;
Rough pioneers who lead the sylvan war
And nature's deepest solitudes unbar,
And scatter where the wild beasts make their den,
The seeds of cities, and the homes of men.

XV.

In other groups he marks the easy grace,
And lively features of the Gallic race ;
Happy with what the day brings forth, their heart
Ambition proof, ne'er felt th' aspiring smart,
Nor cared to know that in this moving age,
When rival nations in the race engage,
They who stand still, are quickly overthrown,
Rolled underfoot and there unpitied groan.
Oh ! aimiable people ! dare to brace
The rival foot and try the emulous race ;
Nor to the vigorous Saxon idly yield
Without the praise of a contested field !
And yet, have they mild virtues of their own
To their more rugged rivals hardly known ;
Be their's the praise of a contented mind,
Of gentle manners and an air refined ;
Communicative, social, light and gay,
Pleasing and pleased they flutter life away ;
Supremely blest, when Sunday's sunny glance
Calls up the village to the merry dance ;

With mass devoutly heard, in sport and play,
And social feast, they end the holy day.

XVI.

Anon, a different group attracts the eye ;
The last poor remnant of a race gone by :
With sad dejection pictured in his mien,
The Indian slowly moves across the scene.
With cold, incurious view, his eye beholds
The busy scene, while closer he enfolds
His mantle round his breast, and idly sped,
His soft mocassin glides with noiseless tread.
Heirs of a Continent ! by force or guile,
Pushed by intruders off their rightful soil ;
Once mighty nations, shrunk to feeble bands,
Scarce find a corner of their native lands,
Where they may spread their blankets and conceal
The secret griefs, their stoic bosoms feel.

XVII.

O ! wonderous change ! The Huron's once proud band,
That shook the hatchet o'er the trembling land,
Bears venal trinkets round, or feebly spread
Begs of the scornful white a little bread.
Long, long, the hapless Huron rued the hour,
He braved the Iroquois' unsparing power ;
But found the white man's false protection still
More surely than the Indian foeman kill.
And e'en the Iroquois, lords of the woods,
Whose proud canoes triumphant swept the floods,
Now glut the Huron's vengeance with their shame,
And melt like April snows, all but their mighty name !

XVIII.

Quebec, romantic city ! fare thee well !

3

Thy native courtesy rests like a spell
Of sweetest memory, as the traveller leaves
Thy glorious rock, where spotless honour cleaves,
Pure as the floods of light that wash thy walls,
When unobscured the noon-tide splendour falls.
Now Walwyn and his sons again embark,
Where groaning steam impels the wingless ark,
Which like Chimera belches fire and smoke,
While torturing engines writhe with timed stroke,
The circling wheels divide the flashing stream
And soon Quebec fades like a glorious dream.

XIX.

Now as they stem the broad, full flood that pours
Brimming, between the distant sloping shores,
At every turn the strangers' eyes admire
The rural village and the parish spire;
The gay green fields and cots of chalky white,
Backed by the distant woods in summer's livery dight,
The Sylvan God, could he resume his reign,
Through yonder groves might lead his laughing train,
Nor know, while roaming o'er each plain and hill
But in Arcadia's scenes he sported still;
Or if he deigned his mellow reeds to tune
In noon-day shade, or 'neath the beaming moon,
Gay rustics would as blithely tip-toe spring
As ere his pipe led round the mazy ring.

XX.

Anon, the mighty stream, clear as the skies,
Deep, full and flowing, bids their wonder rise.
St. Lawrence! justly chief of all the floods,
That roll through boundless plains and trackless woods,
Let these, their springs and small beginnings prize,
In ocean-lakes thou takest thy royal rise;
With weight of seas, majestically slow,

Thy stately course knows neither ebb nor flow.
The thirsty sun ne'er bares thy yellow sands,
Stranding a nation's wealth on new-formed lands,
Nor wintry floods with raging tumult rise,
Mocking the husbandman's despairing cries,
While flocks and herds and homes go sweeping by;
And ruined fields 'neath one vast deluge lie.
But when chill Winter's frost creeps silent o'er,
And on thy waters lays his crystal floor;
With clanging hoofs thy solid bosom rings,
The fur-clad sledge on burnished runner springs;
From bank to bank, the reunited swains
Hail the vast bridge that joins their sundered plains.

XXI.

But now when Summer pours his dancing beams,
And feathered fowl unnumbered skim the streams,
Each curious art of man is called in play,
And crowds with varied craft the great highway:
The floating palace urged by force of steam,
With Titan's strength impetuous shears the stream,
The sea-borne ship in wonder spreads her sails,
Where new-mown hay perfumes the kindly gales,
The rapid barge, the lightly poised bateau
And e'en the Indian's fragile bark canoe.
Anon, the spacious raft, all finned with oars,
Like some vast field floats past the looking shores,
Bearing the forests down, that once surveyed,
The rude Algonquin 'neath their columned shade.
The startled deer and surly climbing bear,
Unroofed, in farther thickets seek their lair.
Those glorious pines, whose tops the highest grew,
And drank in cloudless heaven the purest dew,
From England's stately decks shall rise sublime
And spread her snow-white sails in every clime,
The world's oppressors trembling as they sweep,
With streaming pennons o'er the subject deep.

Ottawa's pride in rightful duty goes,
To waft Britannia's thunders on her foes,
To bear her glorious flag to every shore,
Where sea-winds whistle and where billows roar,
While o'er the floods her echoing cannon boom,
And friends rejoice, and foes receive their doom.

XXII.

Thus every hour its pleasing tribute throws ;
Some prospect opens, or some story glows :
Perhaps some aged Priest's historic lore
Of Indian wars that swept this peaceful shore ;
When like the sudden thaw of ice-bound floods,
The painted Iroquois burst from the woods,
And the shrill war-whoop's long vibrating swell,
On hapless Sillery like a tempest fell.
Where 'midst their slaughtered flocks, with cross dis-
　　　played,
The dying Pastors for the dying prayed,
Mixed with their blood the solemn rites of death
And shriving others, breathed their own last breath.

XXIII.

Still on and on they pass, till voices call :
Behold the distant towers of Montreal !
The Royal Mountain throned upon the plain,
Looks proudly down on all his wide domain.
Upon his brow he wears a forest crown,
And at his footstool sits his favorite Town ;
Trade's potent Queen, who holds the balance true,
And weighs the wealth of nations passing through.
A noble fleet with braced and furled sails
That drank the saltness of Atlantic gales,
Lies side by side with craft that came afar,
Where Erie tosses 'neath the Western star,
Or farther Huron's crystal waters shine

Round dainty prows that never tasted brine.
With stony front extend the ponderous quays,
And swarming streets pour out their crowds on these,
A mingled multitude from every land,
Whom Commerce summons with her golden wand.
Well pleased the eye surveys the ample homes
Of learning, solid as her granite domes,
While spires of silvery white, (Truth's livery gay)
With upraised finger point the heaven-ward way.

XXIV.

Yet if the Muse act here the honest friend.
Scorning to flatter, when her words commend ;
Nor yet in silence let a blemish pass,
Whose shadow sullies her reflecting glass ;
Then, let her tell, how in these fair retreats
Where wealth and knowledge fill the noble streets,
Men walk estranged, and factious foul debate,
Despising quiet, disturbs the peaceful State ;
And in these modern times renews the rage,
And social jars of England's Norman age ;
While Gallic vanity, and Saxon pride,
Alike in fault, alike the blame divide.

XXV.

Ah ! foolish citizens, what is the prize
For which your hydra-headed factions rise,
Like two fierce panthers fighting o'er a prey
Which e'er 'tis won, the fox hath stole away ?
Have you not learned, 'tis thus, a country's foes,
Mid civil discords strike their surest blows ;
Or is the downfall of a hundred States
Forgot, and all in vain, their warning fates ?
Where senseless party hatred reckless burns,
And struggling factions domineer by turns ;

Weak and divided, all to ruin press,
And curse the land that they were born to bless.
Then why contend ! Think rather of the day,
When side by side in woody Chateauguay,
Mingling your blood and lavish of your veins,
You rolled invasion off your native plains.

XXVI.

Though fair this land, not here did Walwyn stay ;
Far to the West, his course unfinished lay ;
The fertile West, whose boundary ever flies
Before the axe th' advancing woodman plies ;
Where wave on wave, the sons of Britain's Isle,
Spread through the forests, and possess the soil ;
Where England's manly speech is only heard ;
Her laws transcribed and her names transferred,
Which her proud Colonists, on every hand,
Plant as memorials of their native land.

XXVII.

Again embarked, the travellers behold
The mighty stream, scene after scene, unfold,
Like some vast panorama's glorious show
That fills expectance in its warmest glow.
Now wide expanded basins nurse the floods
In their broad bosoms, issuing from the woods,
Now tumbling rapids, white with foam and spray
Unbar the mighty river's onward way,
Down shelving steps rough-hewn from Ymer's brawn,
By Thor's great hammer at creation's dawn,
St. Lawrence pours his floods and headlong sped
Down, down he rushes o'er the rocky bed.
With foaming crests a thousand currents sweep
In race impetuous down the shallow steep ;
Now whirling round in eddies white as snow ;
Now mingling rush in one dark glassy flow,

Striking with hideous roars and spouting o'er
Th' opposing rocks rent from the wasting shore;
While overhead, eternal vapours fly
In upward showers, and fill the trembling sky,

XXVIII.

Yet even there, the bold Canadian steers
His daring barge, and close destruction shears;
With steady hand he silent grasps his oar,
And takes the rapids where they deepest pour;
Adown the rushing Sault he swiftly glides
And runs the gauntlet 'mid assailing tides;
Through rocks and shallows winds his rapid way,
While round him howl the water-wolves for prey,
Mayhap' the dark Split Rock with futile wrath
Meets the wild river in its downward path,
Where robed in mist, the evil Oonyak stands
To clutch the voyageur with demon hands,
Or pluck apart the raft, or strike a blow
That beats to fragments the unblessed canoe.
In silent prayer the boatman passes by
The fatal rock, and joy lights up his eye,
As turning sharp aside, the quivering barge
Darts past and soon securely floats at large.
So when the stream of life with sudden check,
Encounters rocks, and threatens instant wreck;
The upright man steers calmly on the tides,
Seeks the right course, and 'mid the danger glides;
With every duty done, he soothes his breast,
And unto Providence confides the rest.

XXIX.

The rapids passed, th' eternal roar is still;
The birch and pine no longer crown each hill;
But nobler oaks and spreading maples throw
Their softer shadows on the earth below;

While westward, ever westward, speeding on
To seek his bourne beneath the setting sun,
The traveller forgets his toil and pain
When the broad river is at peace again;
And he surveys the fertile plains expand
Rich with the verdure of the upper land.
Again St. Lawrence flows with even stream,
Smooth as the music of a lover's dream;
Through waving meads and spreading groves, his tide
Reflects the verdant banks on either side.
Not greener pastures those, the Prophet king
Divinely sang by Shiloh's sacred spring,
Where he lay down forgetful of his woes,
His troubled throne, and Israel's restless foes.

XXX.

Now passed Glengarry's shore, where every face
Strong lined and grave, proclaims her Highland race;
Renowned in arms, their honor as of old
Unsullied, and their faith as virgin gold.
There still is heard the rugged mountain tongue,
And Donald's pipes the Highland reel prolong;
There round the winter hearth, old legends tell
How great Dundee at Killiecrankie fell;
When their brave plaided fathers cried the cry
At once of grief, despair and victory.
Or on Culloden, gory field of fame,
How fell for ever, Stewart's royal name;
When shivered lay the targe and red Claymore;
And thousand loyal hearts were stilled for ever more.
And their descendants yet each virtue fires,
That glowed impetuous in their mountain Sires;
Here Hospitality at close of day,
Throws wide his door and bids the stranger stay;
While simple manners, social, kind and warm,
The shy guest win with ineffable charm.
And prompt to guard the freedom theirs by birth,

The Freeman's sword hangs by the Freeman's hearth,
And oft their ranged dead have sternly proved
Their loyal faith and constancy unmoved.
When thundering War rolled o'er our startled plains,
None drained more prodigal their precious veins;
Nor deadlier aimed the steel, when from our shore
Columbia's routed hosts fled pale before.

XXXI.

Now passed St. Regis' level margin where
The ancient Chapel tolls its bell for prayer,
And blue-robed Iroquois skim to and fro,
Amid the eddies of the winding Sault,
And deftly ply the oar and dart the spear
Amid the finny shoals that hover near.
O, noble river! here but half our own,
T'ween rival states, a mighty barrier thrown;
Flow on in peace, no more condemned to feel
The galling burthen of a hostile keel.
No more, thy frightened echoes fly afar
Repeating wild the clarion notes of war;
But softly murmuring linger round the swains,
Tuning the songs of peace on all thy plains,
Laugh with their mirth, or chime their love-sick woes,
Till setting Venus calls them to repose.

XXXII.

Such thoughts as these in Ethwald's fancy play
While sinks in gorgeous clouds the orb of day.
On Prescott's soft declivities, the lithe
And flowing grass waves deep, ripe for the scythe;
Nature as prescient of his coming, spread
Her tenderest herbs to form his dying bed.
Ah! generous youth! will no prophetic glass,
Reflect the future as you smiling pass?
Does no mysterious thrill vibrating dart

Through thy fond father's wise and loving heart?
Thy tender brother fondling by thy side,
Can no presentiment his laughter chide?
Nor show these little hands, on yonder plain
Reeking with vengeance for a brother slain?

XXXIII.

Ah! no, their guardian angels closely screen,
The future horrors of this lovely scene;
Throw Mercy's veil o'er coming days of woe;
The present grief's enough for man to know.
But Constance! thou afar where starry skies,
Turn on the slumbering world their myriad eyes;
What fearful dreams their horrid vigils keep,
And haggard shapes around thy pillow sweep!
Too anxious maid! love's keen discerning ear,
Inturned in sleep, hears spirits talking near,
Who as they watch her slumbers, wile the hour
With sweet converse of love's unbounded power;
Tell how this sleeping maid was left behind,
Though her betrothed was true as she was kind;
And what should be their fate; how he some day.
Would for his country give his life away;
By death be stricken in his bloom of years,
And leave to her his grave, and love's undrying tears,

XXXIV.

Ungrasped by reason and but half discerned
Their speech, the fount of dreams, to dreams is turned,
And rapt in vision, as her fancy rose,
She saw before her all her weight of woes.
The scene a battlefield, where on the ground,
His life's blood pouring from a mortal wound;
She saw her Ethwald turn his dying eye
From heaven to her, with one regretful sigh;
She rushed to succour, but on every side

Foul mocking shapes repel her and deride ;
Till frantic with despair she shrieked : O, save !
Great God, or let me share my Ethwald's grave !
The holy watchers see her writhe in pain,
Divine the cause and stop delusion's reign ;
Wake her with sudden start ; while thrice she sprang,
And thrice, with Ethwald's name, the roof-tree rang.

Canto Third.

I.

But passing on, the rapid Steamer glides
Smooth as a swan upon the glassy tides ;
A thousand verdant spots on either beam
Glance like the happy isles of Mirza's dream,
And sportive Nature revels wild and free,
As the enchanted maze of some strange melody.
Here, little hills and dales, the eye may scan,
And tiny forests scarce the heighth of man,
There, lofty cedar and the airy pine
And spiry firs their fragile boughs combine.
Around the shores low mossy rocks are seen,
With threads of trickling silver drawn between
While dwarfish promontories stretching round,
Form many a tiny Bay and mimic Sound.

II.

Fantastic nest of Islands· could it be
That nature formed this sweet epitome,
For Oberon and all his elvish train
To colonize and spread their sportive reign ?
The restless tribes of airy Fancy, here
Might find a world to match their tiny sphere ;
Upon thed· prancing steeds might urge the race,

Or backed on humming-birds the gad-fly chase ;
Or when full-moons these little hills adorn,
With puffed cheeks resound the beetle's horn,
To call their friends to trace the Fairy ring,
Till bright Phosphoros back the morning bring,
Aurora ever welcome, but when here,
Her blushing cheek betrays bright Phoebus near ;
Each little isle its balmy incense pays ;
And thousand warblings shake the dewy sprays ;
The timid deer from out their coverts stray,
The spotted fawns in merry gambols play ;
Or peering round if safe from human guile,
Dash through the floods and sport from Isle to Isle,
A scene so wonderous strange, it well might seem,
That Nature formed it of a summer dream ;
Her wakened fantasy with all its powers,
Had vainly toiled to frame these fairy bowers.

III.

Through this fair labyrinth the Steamer speeds
Her long swells rolling o'er the bending reeds ;
Thrice flows the waters on each islet shore,
Through narrow straits resounds their sullen roar,
The bright green alders on the margin side
Shrink from the rushing of the sudden tide,
While every beauteous shadow formed below
Of watery groves that hung with pendant bough,
Is in the rude commotion wildly tossed,
Its beauty scattered, and the mirror lost.
Gigantic Power of Steam ! fit emblem thou
Of iron days and mighty toils below,
When man to earth inverts his searching eyes
And worships Vulcan in a modern guise.
When his imaginings no longer brook
God's comment traced in nature's mystic book,
But as the subtle serpent, seek to be
Wise through the fruit of the forbidden tree,

IV.

A hard material age, that vain would view,
The bright ideals of the good and true ;
They like those shadows, vanish in amaze ;
Before the terrors of its earthly gaze.
An age when Science pours its starry light
Cold, dry and searching as the polar night,
Illuming all the outer spheres of thought ;
Still leaves the heart unwarmed, the soul untaught,
And from its iron throne, usurping rules
The captive remnants of the ethic schools,
And life stripped of its garlands, seems to stand
A naked may-pole in a joyless land.

V.

Long have th' Assyrian hunters, waiting stood,
To snare the pilgrim in the gloomy wood
Where run the paths of life, and every bough,
Hangs full of sophistries ; in outward show,
Fair as the fruit of Sodom, while within
Are dust and ashes and presumptuous sin.
And yet proud Science, boding signs imply
The consummation of they era nigh ;
When thou shalt leap at God's supreme command,
A lion's whelp from Bashan's goodly land,
And rule the bold frontiers of knowledge, thine,
A mighty vassal under Truth divine.
Curbing thy pride, His hand already bends,
To one vast purpose all thy several ends ;
To his celestial chariot, yokes thee down
And crowns thee with a glory not thine own.
For lo ! thy months are full and from the maze
Breaks forth the birth of newer, better days.

VI.

The age of Brass, so long in vain foretold,

Shall springs of human sympathies, unfold,
As yet but only dreamt of, by the mind
In secret converse with angelic kind.
The silver beam of Truth's uncovered day,
Shall then pour in its purifying ray,
Illume the dark recesses of the soul
And show to nobler men a nobler goal.
The silver age shall thus awhile adorn,
And usher in at last the golden morn;
The morn when that all-hallowed sun shall rise,
With seven-fold glory in the cloudless skies,
And in its holy, vast, resplendent ball,
Reveal the presence of the Lord of all.
A voice as of the waters shall proclaim
New life to nature's universal frame;
And the full end of God's eternal plan:
Salvation and angelic life to man.

VII.

In that ripe age Philosophy shall shine
Transfigured in the robe of Truth divine;
And duteous Science as a hand-maid wait
T'' unfold the leaves of Heaven's argentine gate;
That gate whose hinges utter softest strains,
As they disclose the true Elysian plains,
Radiant with life, where flowers forever blow,
And carol birds in Morn's unending glow.
Where Wisdom crowns the cup of truth divine,
And pours libations of the Holy Vine;
While Charity, at once infant and sage,
With golden crook leads on the perfect age.

VIII.

At length emerging from the Thousand Isles
A sea-like horizon before them smiles;
And calm outspread in heaven's own azure bright

Ontario's vast expansion sweeps in sight.
Its placid bosom now as smooth as glass,
Reflects each varied object as they pass.
Beneath the wooded shores, depicted clear,
Inverted groves and pendant banks appear ;
The wandering cloud that spots the summer sky,
The graceful schooner gliding slowly by,
The hovering gull, and circling swallow there
Survey their image in the downward air.
A glorious mirror ! polished smoothly o'er
And framed immense within the verdant shore,
So vast and clear all heaven might stoop and view,
Its beauties, pictured in their native hue.

IX.

Armed at all pointt with many a rampart crowned,
Fort Henry guards the Midland classic ground,
Where ancient Frontenac first raised its walls,
And loyal Kingston built her stately halls,
And locks within her deep and noble bay
Our country's hope and trust, in danger's day.
But speeding on the dashing Steamer ploughs
The saltless waters glittering 'neath her bows;
The land fades out of view, and night and day
Still Westward, ever Westward speeds her way.

X.

Now in the distance, o'er the placid lake
Toronto's uplands, the horizon break.
Her spires and turrets tipt with morning rays,
Loom clearly forth above the misty haze,
That sheets her noble bay, and hides her strand,
Rich with the commerce of the Western land.
In academic groves, there Learning draws
Our generous youth to study Wisdom's laws,
To fill their quivers full of arrows bright

And arm them for life's coming arduous fight.
There, Legislation holds her high debate;
And Freedom stands the guardian of the State;
In spotless ermine, Justice sits supreme,
And lifts the scales of law with even beam.
While rich in future hopes, in memories past,
Toronto's glorious destiny is cast;
Mid rival cities of our land I ween
Is hers the Crown, and she the rightful Queen.

XI.

But Westward still they speed; at length the band
Again set foot upon the welcome land.
With lightsome step they trace the hilly ground,
That margins fair Ontario's western bound.
'Twas summer now, and o'er the shady way,
The birds sing welcome and the squirrels play,
Deep forests echo back the jarring wheels
And cheerful hope the weary distance steals.
From the hill-top, a vision greets their eyes
That often seen, still strikes with fresh surprize;
Where in the lap of mountains, gently spread
Proud Lake Ontario rests his glorious head;
Embracing in his arms, the winding strand
And deep recesses of the yielding land.

XII.

Around the curve of hills, green woods ascend.
Trees above trees their various foliage blend,
While sunny glades becheque the mountain side,
That many a league sweeps round in Sylvan pride,
An amphitheatre scooped by the hand
Of giant Nature from the lofty land;
As if for Gods to sit and view the show
Of Titans wrestling in the plain below;
Or scarce less mighty in th' arena scan
The labours of their emulous rival, man.

XIII.

There fresh in youth, with oaken garlands crowned
A rising city spreads her robes around;
Her suburbs still advancing, she again
Extends her arms and grasps the vacant plain:
Till growing ever, lo ! the urban shade
Stands forth the arbitress of taste and trade ;
Where art refines with soft alluring sway
And Fashion decks the city's thoughtless gay ;
While busy thousands by industry thrive,
Like bees still adding honey to their hive.
Marvellous change ! along yon paved way
The Indian war-path ran but yesterday;
And fox and wolf their nightly discord made
Where now resounds the busy hum of trade.

XIV.

Fair spot ! while beauty's thine, let Fame declare
The proud remembrances that linger there ;
And show on Burlington's projecting strand,
The ancient fastness of our Western land ;
Or round yon shouldering hill, where rang the knell
Which echoes yet through every forest dell ;
Where our Leonidas at dead of night,
Brave Harvey, led the patriotic fight,
And 'neath the wooded mountain's sombre shade,
Our country's hope—his slender band arrayed
At midnight hour; when pealing 'midst our foes
His ringing bugles, voiced with thunder, rose,
Dreadful as judgment, while red fires alight
And flashing guns illume the vengeful night.
The tents o'erturned expose a swarming throng,
Crouching beneath the bayonet's glittering prong';
In hideous chorus join a thousand cries ;
Death-shrieks and calls for mercy, rend the skies;
Till Stony Creek, its banks with crimson laved,
And morning dawned and saw our country saved.

4

O'erwhelmed in piteous rout, Columbia's host
Broke like a ship upon an iron coast,
And rent to fragments, 'mid the tempest's roar,
Strewed with its wreck and cumbered all the shore.

XV.

Thus Walwyn travelled on, until the day
Stooped in the West and shed a milder ray.
In aërial seas the floating clouds unfold
Their curly fleeces edged with fringe of gold.
Along the tree-tops shoot the streaming rays
And fire the woods with unconsuming blaze;
The lowing kine the homeward pathway throng,
And piping birds begin their vesper song;
While lengthening shades, their day-time coverts leave
And strike the dial point of dewy eve.

XVI.

Cool in the dusk of the declining day,
A grass-grown path strikes from the beaten way,
And where the matted boughs o'erarching hang
The toiling waggons turn with heavy clang.
Traversed the winding path, the strangers spied
A shallow brook through leaf-choked channel glide,
Tinging the pale wood-grass with deeper green,
And with its murmurs lull the drowsy scene.
No cypress there cast down its funeral shade,
Nor the dank elm its Siren boughs displayed,
Nor dusky tamaraks in phalanx grow
Guarding the morasses that quake below,
But stately oaks, and polished beeches stood,
And ragged hickories, gypsies of the wood,
The ash and dark brown chestnut there were seen
And the rich maple clad in brightest green,
Blest tree! whose juices liquid honey run
Sweet as the cane that waves 'neath India's sun!
While here and there vast fallen trunks reclined,
With upturned roots to slow decay resigned.

XVII.

Long twisted vines their slender cables throw,
Binding the tree tops to the earth below,
And upward, upward, climb their devious way,
Till in the sunshine clear, their tendrils play.
The proudest oaks wear a Bachannal crown,
And lift aloft bright clusters not their own,
With vigorous arms sustain the pliant vine,
And nurse the wilding sprays of future generous wine.
A scene it was in native wildness grand,
Whose dark luxuriance festooned all the land;
And scarce the flashing sun-beams struggled through
The sea of foliage waving to and fro,
While save the gentle rustling of the trees,
The brook's low murmur, or the hum of bees,
Deep silence reigned so still, it pains the ear
And filled the mind with strange and vacant fear.

XVIII.

This forest scene then, was the destined place,
By Walwyn fixed to run his future race,
Replant his hopes, by fate no longer marred,
Bestow his toils and reap his just reward.
Hard by a gushing spring, the waggons staid;
Unyoked, the oxen graze amid the glade,
And soon the nimble youths a fire prepare,
And spread upon the ground their simple fare.
Moved with emotion deep, old Walwyn stood
And gazed long upon the mighty wood,
That seemed to frown defiance, and proclaim
No power of man that wilderness might tame.

XIX.

Sadly he gazed, while memory backward flew,
To Swaledale's meadows gemmed with morning dew:

Where fragrant breezes fanned the blooming lea,
And birds sang gaily, perched on every tree;
Where snowy flocks upon the hill-sides strayed,
And glossy herds reposed beneath the shade ;
And rural life found pleasure in its toils,
Where heaven and earth rejoiced in mutual smiles.
And when from thoughts of these, he cast his eyes
Upon the savage scene that round him lies,
In reason's spite, a momentary chill
Fell on his heart and shook his steady will.

XX.

The task's too great for me ; he sadly said,
With fifty winters' snows upon my head.
Heart-sick he turned, but deigned not to betray
Th' oppressive thoughts that in his bosom lay.
And yet, he cried, 'tis weakness to complain ;
What man has done, that, man may do again ;.
'Neath Labour's hand, these forests will reveal
The virgin soil, their gloomy shades conceal ;
Will turn to fields as fair and green as those,
And treasured mines of rural wealth disclose.

XXI.

Beneath a spreading oak, with solemn care
The little band knelt at the hour of prayer ;
With heartfelt words old Walwyn's lips implored,
With humble gratitude they thank the Lord,
Who through a thousand perils watched them all,
And brought them safely to their destined gaol.
He prayed their heavenly Father's tender grace
Might ever guard them in this lonely place,
And if it pleased kind Providence, to bless
Their labours and the frowns of Fate redress.
O'er his dear sons the earnest Father bowed
His gushing heart in tenderness o'erflowed,

From Truth's straight paths besought them ne'er to
    stray
Nor idly loiter in the sluggard's way;
But every duty duly so pursue,
That God and man approve of all they do.

XXII.

He rose in happier mood; a pleasant calm
Spread o'er his mind and poured a soothing balm.
In gorgeous church or savage wilderness,
He felt that God was there, alike, to bless:
Mid crowded thousands, or where two or three
Call on his name and humbly bend the knee.
All cheerful then they sat them down to share,
Their frugal meal and then for night prepare;
When barked the watchful dogs. A voice was **heard,**
Beneath the trees a stranger form appeared.
An aged man, of stature large and strong,
With upright carriage firmly stepped along,
Who as old Walwyn rose, held out his hand,
With "welcome strangers, to the forest land!
I saw your trail, when crossing through the wood,
And followed thinking I might do you good."

XXIII.

Each took his proffered hand, and meet replied,
In fitting thanks, and much the stranger eyed;
Who with a happy frankness, sure to please
Hearts so congenial, chatted quite at ease.
A simple suit of home-spun grey he wore,
And quilled mocassins on his feet he bore;
While round his waist a wampum girdle tied,
Showed him, perhaps, to native tribes allied.
His looks beamed truth and kindness as he stood
Like some old giant Warder of the wood;
And seventy winter's storms had thickly shed
Th' unmelting snows of time upon his head.

XXIV.

His square and manly features bore upon
Them, marks of fiery trials undergone,
Of passions unregretted, or which still
Held strong dominion in his stubborn will;
For oft his eyes, when former days were named,
Like some old lion's, 'neath his eyebrows flamed,
And showed that years had wrought but small relief
To dim the memories of angry grief.
Yet, much as Fate had warped his noble mind,
He was a man, by nature just and kind,
And frank and truthful, as each hearer owned,
When his deep voice's simple pathos toned.

XXV.

With questions to and fro, and kind replies,
Warm social feelings soon between them rise.
And as the shades of night were gathering round,
The stranger formed their camp upon the ground;
With piles of brush-wood raised an ample shed,
And strewed with hemlock twigs their forest bed,
With crackling logs heaped high the blazing fire,
And bade his hosts his woodman's craft admire.
For many a stirring year, said he, I made
My constant home beneath the greenwood shade,
Though now with peace, content and plenty, blest,
Among my children I enjoy my rest;
To see them happy is my only care,
Their bliss is mine, and that I fully share.
One son alone of all my manly train:
My youngest, Hugh, e'er gives his father pain,
But why repine? I humbly kiss the rod,
And deem that best for me which pleases God.

XXVI.

Roused at his words, sat Ethwald by his side,

With eager questions, fast as he replied;
And when he spake of many a by-gone year,
They one and all pressed closer round to hear.
When wrapt in thought awhile, the aged man
Sat up erect, and thus his tale began:

Canto Fourth.

I.

Strangers, said he, to you who cross the main,
To seek new homes within our wild domain;
You who have seen the garden landscapes glow,
And felt the balmy gales of Europe blow;
Our silent forests' deep and solemn gloom,
Throws on your hearts the shadow of the tomb.
Saw you with my old eyes, these green arcades,
Would far outvie those boasted classic shades;
And in the dusky grandeur of the wood
Your minds content, would seek no greater good.
Full seventy times at least, I now have seen
Fair Spring array the wilds in youthful green,
Where still my aged foot delights to roam,
And leads me wandering days and days from home.
The soothing stillness of these shady walks,
Where safe from harm the deer around me stalks,
Calms down my mind too oft with memories rife,
Of wars and woes that cursed my early life.

II.

Upon the winding Mohawk's level bank,
My father dwelt, and I its waters drank,
Urged o'er its stream, a boy, my light canoe,
And fished its pools and tracked its forests through.
When Childhood passed and youthful strength allowed,

I took to labour, cleared and reaped and ploughed,
While Plenty from the fertile, generous soil
With all things needful yearly blessed our toil.
In early Autumn, fields of golden grain,
Waved like a sea upon the level plain,
Our flocks and herds in richest pastures grazed ;
And strangers oft our goodly coursers praised,
To crown the whole ; domestic love at home,
Brought peace and comfort to our favoured dome ;
When manhood's robust years I first attained,
I wed a maid who long my heart had chained ;
A maid as rich in soul as beauty's charms ;
Who gave three tender children to my arms,
Taught me to feel a father's earnest love,
And all my earthly hopes with them inwove.

III.

But bliss like mine, for earth, was all too great :
Dire discords rocked the land, and rushing Fate,
In furious factions all our people ranged ;
And friends to bitterest foes forever changed.
I sought but truth and right ; I was a man,
When first those loud complaints of wrong began,
I loved my king, and boldly dared despise,
Their factious tales, and base disloyal lies.
For we had lived an honest country-life,
Apart from towns and politics and strife ;
Felt no oppression, and perceived no ill,
That peaceful means might not redress at will.

IV.

My part, at once I took, soon as I saw,
Their last designs were to subvert the law,
Cut off old kindred's kind connecting band,
Dethrone their King and rule the conquered land.
So when the war broke out, I was a man,

Marked out for vengeance by the rebel clan.
Expelled from home, I joined with hundreds more,
The royal flag which gallant Johnson bore;
With them took to the woods, and backward drew,
Till on Canadian hills our standards flew.
But found not rest; for daily to our ears,
Fresh news came in, and stirred our darkest fears.
Our wives and children, needful left behind,
Turned out in woods with cold and hunger pined
Our fields destroyed, our home-steads burnt, while still
Fell rapine raged, and murder worked its will.

V.

Words cannot paint the storm of rage and woe,
That wrought our souls to anger's reddest glow,
While still fresh refugees came in, and all
Confirm the tale and with new griefs appall.
Our numbers swelled, for hunted thus from home
Thousands of banished men the deserts roam.
Wrath heated wrath and sharpened every tongue,
Till all the camp with cries of vengeance rung;
And in a solemn council 'twas ordained,
We should return and rescue what remained.

VI.

Green are the oaken groves and haw-thorn shades,
Round Fort Niagara's walls and pallisades;
Whose war-worn bastions rising from the lake,
The moaning surf's eternal heaving, break.
Its ancient windows looking o'er the plain
Glared with the camp-fires of our martial train;
While all night long the Indian drum afar,
In measured cadence beat the note of war.
'Twas in the month of leaves, in latter May,
When from Niagara we marched away;
As brave a band as trod the woodland soil,

Steeled to endure each suffering, want and toil.
And needful thus; for 'tween us and our foes,
Three hundred miles of trackless forests rose;
Swift rivers crossed our path, and marshes spread
Around our sinking steps, their oozy bed.

VII.

In single files arranged, our march began,
And Indian scouts before the columns ran,
While not a drum beat as we sternly trod
The war-path beaten on the forest-sod.
Ah! faithful Chiefs, and loyal men were there,
Whose hearts' true greatness was beyond compare;
Who through the worst extremities, remained
True to the King whose cause they well sustained.
There, knightly Johnson held the chief command;
And fiery Butler led his Ranger band,
And good Sir Guy; and Brandt, dread of his foes,
Great Chief at whose command six nations rose;
While many a painted warrior of his train,
Close round our march and rigid watch maintain.

VIII.

In silence thus we traced the mighty woods,
Dark as the cloud, wherein the whirlwind broods;
Which all unwarning bursts, and strews the land,
With wide destruction spread on every hand.
Attained the broad frontier, we staid within
The forest's skirts, impatient to begin,
While scouts ran out and spied the doomed vales,
Counted their strength, and brought the faithful tales.
Then like a thunder-bolt among our foes,
On the grey morn, our sudden war-whoop rose,
Prolonged and shrill; while kindling fires around
With horrid glare lit the contested ground.

IX.

In vain their numbers—Fast on every side,
The death-shots rattled and loud yells replied;
While neighbors, friends no more, in conflict met,
And the green earth with kindred blood was wet.
Their block-house stormed, glared like a cave of fire
Where Furies met and wreaked their mutual ire,
And fought and burned, till with an earthquake's bound
The magazines exploding rocked the ground.
'Mid issuing streams of fire, the walls were torn,
And friends and foes in clouds and thunder borne
Aloft in air, 'mid wreck of flying towers
And flaming beams, and sparks, that rose in hissing
        showers.
A moment's silence fell, but soon again
The storm of battle swept along the plain,
As through the vales we rushed, to gather in
Our scattered friends, and venge our murdered kin.

X.

But I felt more the father, and I ran
Swiftly before to where I life began.
Love sped my steps, and oft my arms astart,
In fancy claspt my children to my heart.
Through woods and brakes, by secret paths I pressed,
Straight as the wild bee winging to its nest;
And reached the well-known spot by noon's high day,
When what a scene, O God! before me lay!
All my enclosures levelled to the plain;
Broke down and trampled lay my fields of grain;
And where my home had stood in peace profound,
A heap of blackened ruins strewed the ground.
My eye-balls froze with sudden horror glazed,
Cold tremours shook me as I stood and gazed,
While in my ears, with sad foreboding knell,
My throbbing heart beat like a muffled bell,

Within the walls I rushed, and everywhere,
Ran wildly round, and searched with fierce despair;
I called their names, while Echo only rung
In mockery back, the accents of my tongue:
Till stepping sudden, o'er a charred sill,
I saw a sight! Great God! I see it still!
My wife's, my sire's, my children's tiny bones,
Lay strewed and scorched, 'mid ashes, blood and stones!

XI.

Headlong I fell, and hours I know not, swooned;
And when I woke, my comrades stood around;
With tearful eyes of pity soothed my woe,
Taught me to live, and named the caitiff foe.
My aged father had refused to wear
The rebel colours, and his king forswear.
For this, a band that shamed their human birth,
Surprised and shot him on his friendly hearth,
My helpless family bound, and with acclaims,
Barred up the doors and left the house in flames.
Ah! stranger friends! whose lives have passed afar,
From all the cruel hell of civil war,
What could I do? my soul with madness raved,
Revenge, revenge alone, my spirit craved.
I donned the costume of the Indian race,
And with the war-paint hideous stained my face,
Then drew the hatchet and the scalping knife,
And never, never, spared a rebel's life!

XII.

Joined to a band of men whose wrongs and grief
Were great as mine, I ranged a Forest Chief,
Smoked with the red man round the Council-fire,
And danced the war-dance with extatic ire.
Through all the vast frontiers, from rocky Maine
To glowing Carolina's balmy plain,
We broke new paths and pierced the mighty wood,
Made Death our sport and washed our wrongs in blood,

Let Cherry Valley and Wyoming long
Lament their treason, and repent their wrong ;
That they relentless off like outlaws drove,
And forced us wild in desert woods to rove.
Let red Oriskany bewail the day,
We bore the shattered palm of strife away ;
And many a field beside of blood and fame,
That trembles still to hear the Ranger's name.
From camp to camp, wherever danger drew,
Or battle storm the Royal standard blew,
We crowded in and ranked our bold array,
And revelled in the thickest of the fray.
At other times divided, wide and far,
We carried on a predatory war ;
Surprized posts, and many a scouting band,
And scalping party swept from off the land.

XIII.

Here let me tell a tale, a deed repeat,
Of vengeance sweeter than the choicest meat.
One day encamped in the sombre wood,
An Indian runner swift before me stood ;
Brought tidings, he had seen a heavy trail
Of white men lie along a distant dale.
Said he—The Long Knives travel to the North—
And on the path twice twenty men go forth—
Fierce Woodworth leads the predatory band—
I saw his foot-mark on the yellow sand—.
Woodworth ! I cried, most hated of my foes,
He who contrived and wrought my bitterest woes ;
My father's slayer, and whose demon ire,
My wife and children burnt in cruel fire !
Half mad with joy, I vowed a vow on high,
To take his scalp or in the effort die ;
And like the utterance of a thunder cloud
My band renewed the oath with shouting long and loud,
But far towards the hills of Chateauguay,

The foe was gone and pathless was the way;
And half a moon at least, we must pursue,
Ere we could hope to trap the murdering crew.

XIV.

We numbered fifteen men; But men who stood
Unmatched 'mid all the warriors of the wood:
To track a foe, or lay an ambush right,
Or hand to hand close grapple in the fight.
There stood Oneida Joseph, pensive Chief,
Who sought in war a solace for his grief,
Whose village burnt, and tender wife was slain
With outrages that vilest manhood stain.
Swift-footed Thayenda of Mohawk race,
Who oft outran the bison in the chase;
And brave Santages, whose keen eye alone
Could trace a footstep on the naked stone.
The rest were white men, who to Indian arts,
United giant strength and steadfast hearts;
Whose butchered kindred haunted every face,
And cried for vengeance on the traitor race.

XV.

Bold Waltermeyer, unwearied as the sun,
He smiled only when the fight begun;
No joys, but Warfare's in his bosom spring
Love to a murdered maid and duty to his king;
Lithe Servos, mindful of his father's fall
On his own hearth-stone, 'neath th' assassin's ball;
No foot than his, to battle lighter sped,
No hand more heavy when a traitor bled.
Hawk-eyed Clement, deep skilled in woodland strife;
Who kept Death's tally, marking life for life;
McDonald, Frey, and Middaugh, loyal men,
Whose iron hands crushed many a rebel den;
Who night and day, unceasing went and came,

No peril daunted, and no toil could tame ;
Who from Ontario to Savannah's shore
Kept the revolted land in terror and uproar.
Then one and all, with acclamations ran,
Prepared their arms, and soon our march began.

XVI.

Two days we travelled, ere we reached the dale,
Wherein our scout had seen the beaten trail.
We search the marks with keen inspecting view.
And all declare his joyful tidings true.
With nerves new-strung we started on our way,
Keen as the blood-hound following up his prey ;
Which snuffs the ground and warms in full career,
While hotter lies the scent as swifter flies the deer.
Santazes, subtle Chief I led first the chase,
And step by step picked out the feeble trace ;
He turned the leaves, and viewed each looseued stone
And numbered every foeman one by one.

XVII.

Thus ten long days we swiftly tracked the foe,
And ten long nights we watched for morning's glow,
When food ran out and biting hunger came,
To break our strength and end pursuit in shame.
But fiercer in our breasts than famine, raged
The burning thirst of vengeance unassuaged.
We looked on Woodworth's foot-mark by the way
And nought but death could bar us from our prey.
We still pressed on, and hunger's cravings lulled,
With buds and green leaves from the forest pulled.

XVIII.

Thus five days more, we followed swiftly on
Consumed by want, by toil almost undone ;

When joyous vision ! from a rocky brow,
We spied them marching in the vale below.
Our strength revived, our hearts rose at the sight,
And every eye glowed with a fierce delight,
While silently, our guns we charge with care,
Make loose the hatchet and for fight prepare.
Around the woods, a circle wide we drew,
And got before them where thick bushes grew ;
And by their path on either side the glade,
With crafty care we formed our ambuscade.
Bent to the earth we stooped, and as they came,
Each one picked out his own peculiar aim ;
Woodworth was mine, the leader of the band
The doomed victim of my own right hand ;
And scarce my glowing fury let me lay,
Soon as I saw him in the narrow way.

XIX.

Supinely on they marched, with rifles slung,
And knives and hatchets at their girdles hung ;
Fringed hunting shirts and hairy caps they wore,
And on their limbs gay Indian leggins bore,
We knew at once, they were, in such array,
A scalping-band in search of human prey.
Eager we watched, couched in the spiry grass,
Silent as death and let the foremost pass ;
Till Woodworth came, when like the lightning's dart
I shot the burly ruffian through the heart.
This was the signal ; every rifle rung
Sharp from the grass, from which we instant sprung ;
And with a whoop, that rocked the very wood,
The whoop of death, that chills the bravest blood,
Like panthers sprang we on the staggering foe,
And took a traitor's life at every blow.

XX.

On every side, fierce execrations rose

With Tories ! Rebels ! names, each cursed their foes ;
While swift the reddened hatchet rose and fell,
And ceaseless pealed the dreadful Indian yell ;
But soon the conflict ceased, and strewn around,
Their ghastly corses pressed the trampled ground ;
Dark Woodworth's scalp down from my girdle hung,
And loud and long the shouts of victory rung.

XXI.

But with subsided strife, our starving band,
Spent with the conflict, scarce could upright stand ;
When to their packs for food we eager run ;
And found maize cakes, and meat parched in the sun.
And many a precious trinket there concealed,
Was to our horror stricken eyes revealed.
Among the rebel's spoil, ah ! there I found
The holy ring my Gertrude's promise bound ;
The well-known corals that with merry glee,
My babe had tossed, while dandled on my knee.
From Woodworth's pouch I drew the relics dear,
And pressed them to my lips with many a tear.
Then on his face I turned the felon o'er,
And found his knapsack filled with reeking gore,
But mad with rage and hunger, took the bread
Stained with his blood and spitefully I fed ;
While many a bitter jest was bandied round,
As we sat feasting on the conquered ground.

XXII.

Then we withdrew, and with our trophies came
Back to the camp preceded by our fame ;
The Indian bands flocked in from every side
And met us by Oneida's silvery tide.
The festal fires were lit, and seated round
On shaggy skins that carpeted the ground,
The dusky warriors listened grave and bland,

5

While passed the calumet from hand to hand.
Then at the war-post standing, one by one,
Our march we told and feats of valour done ;
Till I the last arose, while stained with gore
Fierce Woodworth's scalp my griping fingers bore.
I struck the painted pillar till it reeled,
Grief and revenge my childless bosom steeled ;
And as I told my tale, and trophy showed,
Nee! Good! in thunder tones, burst from th' approv-
    ing crowd.

XXIII.

At night, the Indian fife with shrill refrain,
And sullen drums inspire the martial train.
The plumed warriors dance in solemn ring
While Mohawk tongues our brave achievement sing ;
And as with measured step they beat the ground,
Shrill ever and anon the victory shouts resound.
Then came the feast, and last, upon the green,
The thrilling war-dance closed the boisterous scene.
In hideous colors painted black and red,
With tufts of gorgeous feathers on their head,
The warriors danced, while hollow drums resound,
And lead the mimic war in circle round.
Upon their limbs in fringed leggins gay,
Dry rattles hang and harsh dissonance play,
While troops of women near, in dusky bands,
Shriek as the dance goes round and clap their hands.

XIV.

Santages subtle Chief! first bending low,
Seemed round the ring to urge his swift canoe,
While all the rest in fancy, sweep the floods,
Or trace the hostile path across the woods.
When spied the foe, they seem to creep in grass,
And round and round in breathless silence pass,

Till at the onset, loud as roars of hell,
In dreadful chorus burst the dreadful Indian yell,
Wild flash in air the spear and brandished knife
And all the plain shook with the fancied strife;
While ever and anon the scalp-halloo,
Told what the vengeful warriors wont to do.
Thus long they danced and mimicked war's alarms,
And as they turned they shook their glittering arms;
And still their dire halloos they shout amain,
And still with stamping foot beat down the plain.
Till all enflamed with the mimic strife,
Next morn they rose to act it to the life.

XXV.

The Indian camp broke up, for tidings came,
Of distant battles and new fields of fame.
A hundred long canoes launched from the woods,
And dipt their sides in fair Oneida's floods;
And o'er the burthened waves to victory bore
The gathered tribes of many a savage shore.
A thousand dipping paddles threw the spray,
In silvery showers and spangled all the way;
And glittering spears in clusters like the stars.
Shone hungry, bright and greedy for the wars,
While the red warriors song rose wild and loud
And frequent chorus joined from all the martial crowd.

XXVI.

Ah, strangers! thus, for seven long years my life
Was one perpetual scene of bloody strife.
For seven long years I hardly thought a thought
But what a soldier's duty grimly taught.
My heart though clear of base unmanly crimes,
Was greatly changed in those disastrous times;
And I who oft my rifle would not raise,
But pitying let the deer unconscious graze;

Now saw my hand unsparing point the dart,
And strike it vengeful through a human heart.

XXVII.

Such trials steel our souls; outlawed, proscribed,
Reduced to beggary, by traitors gibed
With every insult, tortured, chained and banned,
For our fidelity to king and land;
My hand grew harder, as my childless head,
Was heaped with wrongs might raise the very dead;
And I avenged them. And if e'er my king
Command the trump of war anew to ring,
These aged hands would still his cause maintain,
And all they did before, would do again!

XXVIII.

But Peace at last approved the Rebels' cause
And gave them rest and independant laws.
With heavy hearts we got the king's command
To stay the war and leave the ravaged land;
We wept to hear our drums unwonted beat
Before our serried ranks a slow retreat;
Those drums so often heard, when levelled low
Our charging bayonets drove the yielding foe.
With furled colours and with bitter pains
We left, for ever left, our native plains,
In wilds, where stiil old England's standard flew,
To plant new fields and build our homes anew.

XXIX.

Our gracious king bestowed with bounteous hands,
Rewards, and freely gave Canadian lands,
Where, soon new homesteads everywhere arose,
And peace and plenty brought us sweet repose.
My native cheerfulness returned apace

And long-forgotten smiles illumed my face.
In time, again I wed a virtuous wife,
And led with her a long and happy life.
With children blest, with age's reverence crown'd,
We live among them settled all around,
In our old days rejoiced, to see the grand
And rising glories of our Forest land.
Such, stranger friends, is my true tale of yore,
And that of many a dweller of this shore,
In whose brave sons and daughters live the fires
And loyal spirit of their hardy sires,
And who successive will confirm the good
Old pledges sealed with their fathers' blood.

XXX.

The old man stopped, and silent viewed the fire
In keen remembrances of ancient ire ;
And deeply sighed, while sunk in thought profound
His foot pressed heavy on the leafy ground.
Old Walwyn saw, and sadly sighing said :
Such are the woes from civil warfare bred.
When party madness breaks fair Concord's wand,
And strangles law with brutal, bloody hand.
Woe to the State that lets domestic jars
Grow to a head and burst in factious wars ;
Wars that break up the heart and every good
Of life and happiness defile with blood.
Of all the ills belched out of deepest hell ;
Of all the woes that suffering man can tell ;
Type of the deed of Cain, by God accursed,
Is civil feud and war the very worst.
Vain is the victory, the strife abhorred,
When furious factions draw the hostile sword,
When sad success on battle's groaning plain
Boasts of its triumph over brothers slain,
From age to age the upas tree of death,
Will spread its boughs and breathe its poisoned breath,

The eternal gangrene of the eating sore
Will gnaw their severed hearts for evermore.

XXXI.

Their guest assented, and ere long his mood
Of stormy recollections fell subdued,
With potent, self-control he calmed his mind,
By nature much to cheerfulness inclined;
A man who hated wrong and loved the right,
But militant, for Truth preferred to fight.
He took young Eric playful on his knees,
Fondled the boy and soon was quite at ease,
While cheerful talk prolonged the social hour,
Till night fell heavy on their forest bower.
He then arose and smiling kindly said;
'Tis late; let me prepare a Ranger's bed,
You pitied all our toils and troubles, true,
But in the woods, we had our comforts too.
Upon their couch he spread their blankets neat,
And to the fire he bade them turn their feet;
For thus the red man lies, and safe from pain
Averts his head and slumbers on the plain.
Then to himself he murmured low, and said:
This good old man but ill becomes this shed;
I'll warn our neighbors; and to-morrow night,
'Neath his own roof we'll welcome him aright.
Then piled their fire with logs to last till day,
And bade them all good-night and went his way.
His parting footsteps die upon the hill,
And through the midnight forest all was still.

Canto Fifth.

I.

Now morning dawns and kindling skies illume
The beauteous woods that yield a soft perfume;

The rising sun's first breath, a freshening breeze,
Stirs all the glittering net-work of the trees;
The leafy hosts respond with solemn sound
And shake their dew-drops pattering on the ground,
Awake the Strangers to their morning prayer,
And with them praise the great Preserver's care.
All were afoot; but scarcely had the sun,
Rolled up his orb and bright the day begun,
When distant voices echoing cheerily round
Through the cool forest's leafy aisles resound.
Soon Ranger John approached and nigh at hand,
Of robust swains appeared a numerous band;
The hue of health their hardy features wore,
And glittering axes on their shoulders bore,
While yoked oxen trailing chains along,
Push through the brakes and all the pathway throng.

II.

Their salutations over—fain to know,
Old Walwyn asked what meant this morning's show?
When Ranger John spoke as he took his hand:
Such is the custom of the Forest land;
A worthy stranger in our woodlands come
To live among us and erect his home;
Brings pleasure to the old: joy to the gay,
And to our youth a merry holiday.
And know our rural holidays, in truth,
Are days when we unite our jovial youth,
For some strong labour that craves common aid,
And which by after sports is well repaid.
To day we come to take you by the hand;
And make an opening on your timbered land;
And raise a house wherein by fall of night,
Your own free hearth may welcome you aright.

III.

Then to their task the young men gaily sprung,

And sharp and quick the biting axes rung;
And soon the reeling forest bowed its head,
And crashing trees their lofty honours shed;
While toiling oxen drag the spoils away,
And bare an ample circle to the day.
Old John walked through the midst, the soul of all,
Who worked obedient to his boisterous call;
Some hewed the logs; some shaped with nicer eye;
While some strong-handed raised them up on high,
Notch fitting notch, till pleasant in the wood,
An ample cabin in the clearing stood.

IV.

Their labours done, a plenteous feast was spread,
And mirth and jollity their radiance shed;
The foaming flaggons temperately they taste,
For pastime calls them and they rise in haste.
With pleased looks and criticising tongue,
The elders stand aside and watch the young,
Who stripped, with friendly challenges proclaim,
Their skill in wrestling, and opponents name.
When many a bout was tried, who should own
Among them all the victor's proud renown.
Young Ethwald who had laboured with the best
Stood by the elders to observe the rest.
Nor wished, though pleased to see, the sport to share,
For pensive and retiring was his air.
Although his figure tall beyond his age,
Agile and strong seemed fitted to engage;
And from the manly game bear off a prize,
And win a name esteemed in youthful eyes.
Now were these tokens false; for well he knew
The subtle arts that more than strength subdue;
And oft mid Swaledale's wrestling shepherds seen,
Had overthrown in turn the village green.

V.

To draw him forth, a burly youth advanced,

And rudely challenged him, and scornful glanced;
Unlike his comrades, whose bright eyes expressed,
The warm good-nature of each generous breast.
This was the youngest-born of Ranger John,
Who long had lived a disobedient son,
Seemed prone to ill, and frequent left his home.
And vagrant round the country loved to roam.
Dark features marked him, and a vicious eye,
Keen, bold and selfish seemed to defy;
His mind acute, his frame of largest size
And skilled in manly games oft bore the prize.
But still his domineering spirit spoiled,
The meed of fame for which he eager toiled.

VI.

Disliked by his fellows, he repined
To see them to a stranger more inclined;
And formed a spiteful plan, whate'er befall
To humble one in favour with them all.
Ethwald declined the strife; though unaware
Of Hugh's intent, nor would their pastime share;
But John insisted, and his father loved
Th' athletic sports that sturdy manhood proved,
While Hugh still pressed, for that the young man's
    name,
Till he gave in, and smiling joined the game.

VII.

Stripped for the strife, when in the midst they stand,
Hugh fiercely griped his young opponent's hand;
His better feelings vainly disallowed
The causeless ire that in his bosom glowed.
Now face to face they turn and sudden clasp,
Each other round and test each straining grasp;
Now feints they try to lax with crafty aim,
The watchful guard and win an early fame;

Or with some new device of art applied,
With feet enlocked they reel from side to side.
Now breathless silence round the ring prevails,
While mastery seems balanced in the scales ;
Now hearty cheers approving fill the glade;
As some fine stroke of skill is well displayed ;
Till Fate with sentence of the future rife,
Declared for Ethwald and cut short the strife.
Upon a rolling stone, Hugh's foot gave way,
And in an instant Ethwald won the day ;
Who, as Hugh staggered, whirled him sharply round,
Tripped up his heels and raised him from the ground,
His quivering foot aloft, a moment fly,
And prostrate on the grass, he angry viewed the sky.

VIII.

Loud shouts applauded Ethwald's strength and skill ;
While Ranger John cried out with right good will :
Rise Hugh, and give the gallant youth thy hand,
Who proves his title to the Forest land.
Let no despite lie heavy on thy heart,
But love him better for his manly part.
Hugh slowly rose, repulsing Ethwald's aid,
And to himself in deep resentment said :
My Father may applaud, grey-headed fool !
So may my brothers, trained up in his school ;
I hate this stranger now, and by this hand
We meet again ere I depart the land.
I hate my home, my country, kindred, all ;
May condemnation blasting on them fall !
For Southern climes where there is gold to win,
By morrow's sun-rise I my course begin ;
And leave these rustics here to till the soil,
And praise the pleasures earned by so much toil.

IX.

Young Ethwald heard his murmurs ; and his mind

Vexed with his victory, more than half repined;
Kindly he spake, for at its topmost flood,
Success had in a moment, cooled his blood.
He reached his hand to Hugh, who struck it off,
With execration deep and bitter scoff.
Old John's keen eye flashed lightning, and his tongue
Spake thunder, as irate he instant sprung.
Hugh! Hugh! desist! what mischief guides thy hand?
The like was never seen in all the land!
What strike the stranger youth? by God's great name,
I blush to own thee, blush for very shame!
Turn I command thee, and repair the wrong;
Ask his forgiveness, or thy Father's tongue
Shall speak a doom will shake thy very soul,
And brand thy forehead like a burning coal!

X.

Hugh trembled as he looked him eye to eye;
But sullen said: your curses I defy;
At your behest, I give him not my hand,
I'm free; and I'll obey no man's command.
To-morrow's sun will see me leave these woods,
For Southern lands, where fortune rolls in floods;
Where daring spirits, men who dare be free,
Defy the laws, and live by mastery;
Free'd from your kingly rule, I there will roam
In golden paths undreamed of here at home.

XI.

The father sprang; his ears could no more brook,
Rage, grief and pity mingled in each look.
Hugh! Hugh! he cried: degenerate of thy race!
My only child who shames his father's face!
Thou go to Southern lands, and leave thy own,
And live an alien to thy Monarch's crown?
Thy father's heart might pardon all beside;

My love rejected, and my will defied ;
Yea, pity and forgive each viler thing ;
But never base desertion of thy king.
Thou knowest me, Hugh ; wert thou the dearest son
That ever Father's heart did dote upon ;
That word spoke in my ears, would seal thy fate,
A child of malediction, wrath and hate.

XII.

What ; darest repeat thy treason ? by this hand,
I'll smite thee to the earth whereon we stand ;
Son though he be—Here Walwyn rushed between,
With earnest intercession pleaded keen,
That Hugh was vexed, by youthful passion led,
Perhaps scarce knowing what he did or said.
He prayed him calm his anger and withhold
His fatal curse unlaunched, till reason cold
Had weighed the cause, when haply to his joy
Forgiveness would restore his sorrowing boy.
The father looked in silent dubious mood,
Seemed to relax, but still dilated stood ;
When Walwyn's little son, in artless wise.
Ran to his knees and looked with earnest eyes.
Said he ; Sir, pardon Hugh, you said last night,
That he when little was my picture quite ;
I sought him out to-day, and told him all,
And he was kind, although so dark and tall.

XIII.

Old John looked down, while in his eyes of fire,
A shade of moisture cooled the glowing ire ;
Collected to a drop, it silent fell
Upon the little face that plead so well.
These artless words of peace his purpose broke;
Awhile he pondered and then calmly spoke :
Hugh, I respite thee for this infant's sake,

And that brave youth's whose worthy heart must ache,
That through him blameless sprung a cause of strife,
That will imbitter all thy future life.
But since to Southern lands, thou meanst to roam,
And leave our peace and freedom here at home;
I'll give thee gifts, thy own peculiar share
Of all my wealth, that thou may'st never dare,
Reproach thy father, that he used thee ill,
Except in yielding to thy wayward will.
Go home, and for thy exile make array
To-morrow's sun-rise sees thee on thy way.

XIV.

Hugh stood subdued, for streaks of goodness still,
Chequered the darker tissue of his will.
Father, he said: forgive my evil tongue,
And heart still worse, to dare so foul a wrong;
My brothers pardon me the grievous shame,
That I have brought upon our honoured name.
Unworthy of your love, I must away;
My mind is ill, and might again betray;
And this strange youth, I give him here my hand;
May he be happy in the Forest land;
A land too peaceful for my wayward life,
Run wild in disobedience, crime and strife.

XV.

All stood with pity moved, and some began
To intercede, and soothe the rash young man.
"He might be moved to stay"—But Ranger John
Spoke calmly: no! tis best he were begone;
Let him to Southern lands awhile repair,
And taste the freedom which he boasted there;
Gather the wealth that rolls in golden floods,
And if he can, despise our peaceful woods.
Go Hugh! prepare thy journey; and until

Thy better thoughts can rule thy evil will;
Return no more, for thy old father's sake,
His peace, yea more, perhaps his heart to break.
In silence, Hugh obediently retired,
While low the sun the Western forests fired;
The assemblage soon dispersed, the sad event
Of Hugh, their minds from farther pleasure rent.
With many kind adieus, old Ranger John
And all the rest left Walwyn and his son;
While hand in hand full many a promise passed,
This marred meeting should not be the last.

XVI.

Young Ethwald left his couch at morning's grey,
And borne on flying feet, pursued his way,
Along a leaf-strown path where couchant deer
Rose as he passed and gazed with sudden fear.
But gazed unheeded; Ethwald's troubled thought,
All night was fixed on Hugh, and now he sought,
The neighboring vale where large mid meadows fair,
His father's mansion breathed the balmy air.
Emerging from the woods; on either side,
A glittering brook, the vale extended wide,
Banked in the distance by a rising ground,
With gorgeous foliage to the summit crowned.
In long succession, massive Farmsteads rose,
And flocks and herds, by distance small, repose;
With driving ploughs afield; and blithe among
The tinkling cows, was heard the milkmaid's song,
And hundred merry notes of morn, that hail
The rising sun throughout the rural vale.

XVII.

Upon the brow of the descending wood
Ethwald entranced, a moment gazing stood.
But soon his thoughts to hapless Hugh return,

As he self-blaming felt his bosom burn,
With shame that through him the occasion fell,
That tempted Hugh unduteous to rebel.
And now he sought them at that early hour
To make all reparation in his power;
Again to intercede, though vain he knew;
But at the least to bid a kind adieu.

XVIII.

He turned in the lane, where eglantine
Clustered the fence and breathed a breath divine;
Where Lombard poplars stood in double row
Turned up their boughs and scorned the earth below,
There sauntered Ranger John, who meeting, said:
Welcome young friend; but why so early sped?
Ah! I divine, you come to see poor Hugh.
He went last night, nor left us one adieu.
May God be with the reckless boy! But come;
You go not back before you see our home.
Grief may be heavy; but my soul disdains,
Such weaknesses as show the bosom's pains.
Then took he Ethwald's arm, and led him through
Sweet smelling orchards glittering with dew;
Where vast his homestead rose, with plenty rife,
And shrill with clarion notes of feathered life;
While lowing kine that crop the grassy vale
Await their turn to fill the milking pail.
The spacious house of solid timbers made,
With walls snow-white, stood in the leafy shade
Of spreading maples, while expanded round,
Parterres of flowers and verdure clothed the ground.

XIX.

As they approached the door, a rosy maid
Looked forth and to her sisters hastily said:
The stranger comes of whom our Father spake!

The eldest? no! or Herman made mistake,
When he described them to us yesternight;
Fair-haired he is and young, with eyes of azure light,
'Tis he who strove with Hugh.   Alas! in vain,
Nor Sire's nor sister's love could ever Hugh restrain.
One maid arose from spinning at the wheel,
And nimbly, one prepared the morning's meal;
While one dark-eyed with dimples in her face,
Sat at the loom and wove with modest grace.

XX.

With health and exercise their features glow,
And eyes look thoughts as pure as arctic snow;
Not lighter than their step the squirrel bounds,
And soft and clear each silvery voice resounds.
Arrayed in graceful robes of russet brown,
Whose neatness shamed the tinsel of the town,
Worthy they seemed to bear Diana's bow
Or set the Hellespont again aglow.
With modest salutation they return
The stranger's courtesies, and briefly learn
The kind intent that brought him, while their eyes
Begin to fill as deep emotions rise;
When Ranger John spake with his usual cheer:
Children! he proved a traitor; not a tear
Should I or you upon the recreant fling,
Who spake as he spake of his land and king.

XXI.

Young Ethwald curious viewed the spacious dome;
The plenteous, cleanly, warm Canadian home.
Massive and strong, each household good displayed
The simple truthfulness their minds arrayed.
Well-cushioned chairs of solid oaken wood,
And heavy tables firm and squarely stood;
While female taste, from needle, wheel and loom

With cheerful drapery adorned each room.
Upon the heavy beams dependant swung
Crooked powder-horns, and well-kept rifles hung;
And by the massive chimney's deep recess,
Huge antlers hold the hunter's sylvan dress.
Upon the table lay with reverent care,
The family bible and the book of prayer;
And duly morn and night a portion read
Composed their minds and blessed their peaceful bed.

XXII.

Religion was with them more deed than word:
To love their neighbor and to fear the Lord;
Honour their king and yield his high degree,
The loyal trust and homage of the free.
Their sober minds with healthful vigour blest,
The best of knowledge, how to live, possessed;
Unspoiled by sophistry, and clear and strong
Their plain good sense was never in the wrong;
While self-earned competence secured by these
Made daily industry a life of ease.

XXIII.

Thus Ethwald saw and mused; when echoing shrill
The morning horn rang sweet o'er grove and hill;
The ploughboys listened on the fallow ground
And trooping home obeyed the welcome sound.
Brave kindred youths who as they turn the soil
Draw health and vigour from the grateful toil.
With welcome smile and warmly clasped hand,
Ethwald was greeted by the friendly band;
While Ranger John with kind insistance led
To share their morning meal and break their bread.
At length they rose and he must haste away;
With warm adieus he took his homeward way;
And long the bright-eyed maidens watching stood
Till he was lost beneath the distant wood.

6

Canto Sixth.

I.

But seasons come and go ; the leaves turn sear
And cooler breezes fan the fainting year.
Now Indian-summers's golden vapours fly
And Nature dreams 'neath Autumn's drowsy eye ;
The changing forests in a gorgeous blaze,
Of glory, end their transient summer days.
The flush of fading verdure, like the streak
Of beauty on consumption's dying cheek,
Paints all the woods, and fills the deep arcades
Of vari-colored leaves, with glowing shades
Serene and holy, as the rays divine
That through the pictured panes of some old Minster
        shine.

II.

The beech and the sycamore in robes of gold,
Await their doom like Egypt's Queen of old.
The spreading chestnut, tints of orange throws ;
And brilliant scarlet on the maple glows.
The prouder oaks blush with a deeper red,
Abashed that they their leafy vestments shed ;
While every glowing tint and shade between,
A flood of glory pours on all the sylvan scene.
But the tall pine, however seasons range,
Clad in eternal green braves every change ;
Yea, as the storms of winter harder blow
Its vigorous branches with fresh verdure glow,
'Mid fading nature rising stern and grand,
The type and emblem of the Forest land.

III.

Now seven times, Aries had clambered nigh

The equal boundaries of the vernal sky;
And seven times yellow-wreathed with corn in ear,
Had Libra, in her balance weighed the year,
Since Walwyn.weary and despondent stood
Beside his camp-fire in the lonely wood.
His unremitting labours, from the ground
Had cleared the forests that enclosed him round;
And year by year enlarging, backward threw
The woody circle that around him grew.
His axes constant rang, and falling trees
With sudden crash resounded on the breeze;
While glaring fires the tranquil night illumed,
And clouds of smoke each rising morrow gloomed,
Till wide and far, a spacious plain was cleared,
Fair meadows rose and bubbling springs appeared;
And flocks, and herds, and yellow harvests came
To bless his labour and restore his fame.

IV.

His sons to youth and robust manhood grown,
Show on their cheeks hale labour's ruddy brown.
Eric, a noble boy, whose ardent blood
Impelled him oft to range the mighty wood;
First in the chase, he turned the flying deer;
And sought the wolf within his cavern drear;
Or singly in the thicket brought to bay
The savage bear, and took his spoils away.
At Sylvan shootings when our youth appear,
And in the midst the feathered targets rear,
Few hunters matched the sureness of his aim
And from his rifle won the doomed game.
When harvest-moons the long-day labours closed,
His ardent soul in further toils reposed,
He called his comrades and with axe and gun
By moonlight chased the nimble, rough raccoon..

V.

Old Ranger John with all a hunter's joy,

Each art of woodcraft taught the stirring boy;
Showed him by night to stalk the wondering deer,
While dazzling torches strike a sudden fear;
And in the dark their glaring orbits flame,
And guide unerringly the hunter's aim.
Oft, mirthful sport, satire on human pride,
To trap wild turkeys forth the hunters hied.
A cage they build with door to let them in,
Lay bait to tempt and watch the sport begin.
The pompous train stalk filing through the wood,
Stoop 'neath the doorway and devour the food,
When safely housed they lift their heads so high.
The silly birds no more the entrance spy;
But clamorous flutter with prodigious din,
While but their folly keeps them fastened in.
To their high-headedness, a foolish prey,
The laughing hunters bear them all away.

VI.

Yet much as Eric, warm with youthful blood,
Loved sylvan sports and ranging through the wood;
True to his duty, when the rising sun
Called him a-field, as blithely forth he run,
As ardently in rural labour sought
To earn the active joys his leisure brought.
No brighter eye than his on maiden glanced,
No foot more sprightly to the viol danced,
The merriest tongue to tell a pleasing tale,
The favorite he, of all th' admiring vale.
Yet, in his gayest flight it was his pride
To let grave Ethwald temper him and guide;
His brother, whom he loved with all the fire,
Esteem and fond affection could inspire.

VII.

Ethwald, sedate and tranquil in his　mood,

His native warmth, by sober thought subdued;
One shining load-star, fixed as the pole,
Steadied his passions and confirmed his soul.
His youthful love by distance undecayed,
By lapse of time, a purer essence made,
Seemed more akin to that which rules above,
Than like the grosser springs that mortals move.
His lovely Constance, plighted of his youth,
For her his heart preserved its early truth;
For her his constant toil, his steady care,
His daily musing, and his nightly prayer.
While every generous thought and lofty aim
Drew life and vigour from the sacred flame.

VIII.

O! wondrous spring of life, when tender, true,
Requited love expels the formless crew
Of fitful passions from the youthful breast,
And sits enthroned in everlasting rest!
Fair woman! she recipient first, of God,
Makes manly hearts to bud like Aaron,s rod;
Prime source below of all the world calls fame
Of all approving angels love to name;
Her smiles with love and approbation fraught,
To every manly deed and noble thought,
Impel the warrior and inspire the bard
At once their motive and their great reward.

IX.

In early morn, while yet the hoar-frost sheen
Crusted his plough might Ethwald oft be seen.
Turning the furrows until veiled Night
Hung in the West her lamp of silver light.
In all his father's rural wisdom taught.
While Ranger John his long experience brought
He learned the seasons and observed with care

The prudent rules, that richest harvests bear.
When Autumn suns in smaller circles moved,
His loamy fallows all his labours proved;
The golden seed of wheat's enriching ear
Was sown and bounteous blessed the coming year.

X.

When vernal zephyrs from the South returned,
And fitful May alternate chilled and burned;
When hazy smokes at morn hang o'er the grounds
And loud at eve the tree-frog's note resounds;
Then all astir, the patient oxen walk,
The ploughboys whistle and the seedsmen stalk,
The toothed harrow hides the scattered grain
And bristling crops soon guard the waving plain.
By Ranger John instructed, when he saw
The white-oak leaves large as a squirrel's paw,
And warm June mornings rise with ruddy haze,
He knew 'twas time to plant the pearly maize,
Whose tapering leaves will soon in pairs appear
And golden kernels in their bosom rear.

XI.

As summer heats begin to parch the air
His panting flocks reclaim his tender care.
Beneath the shade of some old spreading tree
The shepherd takes them on his bended knee;
And plies with nimble hand the sounding shears
About their trembling sides and shrinking ears;
Till light they spring, stripped of their woolly load;
The bleating lambs run scared all abroad;
While on the grass, the piles of fleeces grow,
Like drifts in summer-time of winter's snow.
Now smile the jovial swains at tempests near,
When rise Orion and the Charioteer;
When bright at eve the Northern dancers play;

And Boreas thunders down the milky-way;
Wrapt in their fleecy garb, the swains defy
The blustering terrors of the winter sky.

XII.

In young July when roses bloom and fade,
And chirping insects chorus in the shade;
When merry blackbirds all day tune their song,
And whip-poor-wills at eve their plaint prolong.
When fairy humming-birds with harmless wound,
Search the gay flower-cups where sweets abound,
And whirring fan with ever-beating wing
The ravished rose and tulip's honey-spring.
Sweet time to toil! the sprightly youths repair
Where fragrant meadows scent the loitering air,
And whet their sounding scythes, while dew-drops
    bright
Tip every leaflet with a bead of light.
Advancing in a line the mowers pass,
And busy rakers sweep the drying grass
In fragrant wind-rows, which tossed up again
In hay-cocks over-hillock all the plain.
At noon, the rustic group reposing laid,
'Neath spreading maples dense with cooling shade,
Quaff the bright cider from the social can,
While pleasant jests pass round from man to man.
Some maiden's charms, some couple's wedded bliss;
What crops on that farm, and what herds on this;
Some favorite steed or lover's late disgrace,
Form endless topics for the rural race;
And thus good-humor with her gossip tongue
Chats through the noon-tide hour and cheers the resting
    throng.

XIII.

But when July pours down his parting beams

Burns up the summer days and dries the stream:
The graceful maize unbinds its silky hair,
And tells the legend of the Indian fair.
Bright Mondamin who haply met the eye,
Of Lenape's tall Chieftain roving by;
Her people's foe, who rudely sought to gain
Her maiden hand unwooed, and steps restrain.
And thus the dark-eyed maids of Huron's race
At every green-corn feast, the tale retrace:
Shrieking ran Mondamin, while he pursued
O'er grassy prairie and through leafy wood;
As rang his steps on her dilated ears,
Fresh sprang the maid impelled by newer fears;
She winds, she doubles, while her eyes in vain
Seek aid and refuge on the desert plain.

XIV.

Light footed Mondamin! not swifter flies
The forked swallow through the summer skies;
Not swifter runs the doe, when bays the hound
Fierce in her tracks and tears along the ground,
Than she young virgin, winged with terror sped,
And from the Chief's abhorred embraces fled.
Aye as she ran she shrieked Wacondah's name,
Great Manitou! she cried; avert my shame—
O! save in mercy save, my virgin charms,
And take my life, but keep me from his arms!

XV.

Wacondah heard, and looking from the sun,
Beheld the Chief pursue, the maiden run;
That feebler fell her footsteps on the ground,
While he fresh flushed with hope gained every bound,
Until with forceful grasp he seized his prize;
When shrieked the maid, and lo! before his eyes,
She rooted stood,. and wonderous sight and strange,

To spreading leaves her flying garments change,
A graceful stalk of maize rose in the air,
And from its top waved her dishevelled hair.
While great Wacondah spake the awful word :
Through all your tribes be just, and fear the Lord ;
And ever as you see the tufted maize,
Revere chaste virtue, and Wacondah praise.

XVI.

When August's early suns blazed high at noon ;
And broad at twilight rose the harvest-moon ;
The glorious fields of yellow bending corn,
Called out the reapers by the flush of morn.
With rocking step the hardy cradler throws
His wickered scythe, and down the harvest mows ;
The busy rakers sweep the stubble plain
And bind in lusty sheaves the fallen grain ;
While buried waggons groan beneath the loads
Of nodding grain, that take the homeward roads,
Like moving hills, where perched up on high
Their harvest-home the merry reapers cry.

XVII.

O, happy land ! that seeks in scenes like these,
The harmless pleasures that uncloying please ;
Where Peace and Industry—with sober hand,
Divide the bounty of the fruitful land ;
Where Law's broad aegis guards the sacred soil
And Freedom sweetens all the Yeoman's toil.
Such Canada, my honoured Country, thou !
My theme, my crown, my choicest wish below !
May no strange Gods invade thy happy bowers
And claim the homage due thy native powers ;
May no base feuds distract thy generous mind,
Nor luxury corrupt, nor vice unbind ;
But sacred keep thy virtues and maintain

Thy British Freedom and thy rural reign;
So shalt thou sit enthroned, with glory crowned
From Labrador to Nootka's lonely sound,
And all the boisterous North shall own thy sway,
And Southern stars grow dim beneath thy rising day.

XVIII.

Thus Ethwald tilled the soil, and eye and ear
Observed the tokens of the changeful year.
When humid vapors on th' horizon lay
And heavy banks of clouds engulfed the day;
When pale 'mid watery rings the moon was borne
Or downward turned at eve her dripping horn;
When o'er the Lake's broad bosom, looming clear
The further shore's high wooded heights appear
At morn or eve, and in the lazy air
Laputa's cloudy land seems floating there;
Then knew he well the signs that promise rain
Which speedily will soak the arid plain,
Bring out the swelling buds and full display
The summer-flowers in all their grand array.

XIX.

At other times, when Morn's red arrows gleam,
And smoky vapors blunt the solar beam;
Aurora, ere her veil of mist withdrew,
Tipped every blade of grass with drops of dew;
When gauzy cobwebs net the verdant ground,
And swallows wheel in lofty circles round;
The husbandman with pleasure hails the sign
Of cloudless sunny days that ripening shine;
Of starry evenings robed in silver light,
Of Moons that sail throughout the summer night;
The Moon, mysterious power! that rules and sways
The tide of life through Nature's leafy maze.
While Phœbus warms with life the brooding rain,

She guides it through the vegetable vein ;
Till all the earth arrayed in vivid green
Like Eden glows in every heightened scene.

XX.

In summer days, when piled in masses high,
The thunder-pillars prop the evening sky,
And cloud-land's shining mountains sharp and clear,
With craggy peaks and gloomy dells appear,
As if the far Andes reflected rose,
And pictured in the North their lofty snows.
Forerunner of the storm, the darting ray
Shoots through the clefts, as sinks the orb of day
While flashing fitfully and silent, gleams
The broad sheet-lightning o'er the land of dreams;
And timely bids the reapers gather in
The standing harvest ere the storm begin.

XXI.

But when fierce August suns careering high
Gaze hot and silent from the brazen sky ;
When bird and beast forsake the open glade
And pant all mute within the sultry shade ;
When not a breath doth stir the lightest leaf ;
And springs and brooks dried up deny relief ;
While Nature lies exhausted in the throes
Of parching thirst the sharpest of her woes ;
Then lo ! a small dark cloud all fringed with **red,**
Above th' horizon lifts its livid head ;
Surveys the scene and larger grows to view,
While all the legions of the storm pursue.
The muttering thunder with unceasing din
Proclaims the strife of elements within ;
And lurid flashes flood the murky clouds,
As faster on they follow, crowds on crowds.

XXII.

Eclipsed the sun, his fires at once allayed,
Falls o'er the quaking earth, a dreadful shade ;
A thousand birds aloft in terror rise,
And seek the safest haunts, with piercing cries :
The leaves, they tremble in the breathless woods
And sighing trees confess th' approaching floods.
At once 'mid clouds of dust and flying leaves
The whirlwind sweeps aloft the scattered sheaves ;
Sharp lightning rends the black and marble skies
And thousand-voiced the pealing thunder flies.
The shattered boughs upon the tempest ride ;
And rocking forests groan from side to side ;
While cataracts of rain in deluge pour,
And sweep the smoking land with ceaseless roar.

XXIII.

The wild tornado passes, and the sun
With golden rays peeps through the clouds of dun,.
Green Nature glistens and the piping bird
Within the dripping grove is fluttering heard;
While down the steaming gullies furrowed wide
The rushing waters pour on every side,
And earth refreshed, emerges from the storm
With smiling face and renovated form.
So oft in human life, when Fortune's blaze,
Makes men forgetful of their Maker's praise ;
When through each vein the blood ungenerous creeps
And lethargic each nobler feeling sleeps ;
When hard contracts the soul seduced to ill,
For truth disabled and debased of will ;
Observe kind Providence with holy ire
Send on that man its purifying fire,
Reverses, poverty, disease and death,
To stay corruption's foul contagious breath,
To keep alive the spark of truth within,
Purge off the brute and cleanse the pitchy sin.

XXIV.

God's loving anger, which assailing these
Seeks to assuage the festering soul's disease,
To burst th' infernal chains that bind us fast
And guard our freedom to the very last.
Thus Ethwald ran his rural calm career
Changing his labours with the changing year,
One sole reward he wished to crown his care,
Constance, his homestead as his heart might share.
Social and friendly, yet where youth resort,
Seldom he joined unasked their boisterous sport:
But loved the converse of the wise and old,
And chose with them the pastimes to behold.

XXV.

When harvests all are home and piping loud
November winds drive fast the racking cloud,
The Country Sports begin and changing round,
From house to house the festal nights resound.
As evening nears, from all the neighbouring groves,
The youths and maidens come in merry droves,
The Forest paths re-echo with their glee,
And mirth anticipates the jovial *bee*.
The youths in country suits of homespun grey
Their shapely forms and manly grace display,
A garb, perhaps the busy wheel supplied
Of each dear maid that's tripping by its side.
What wonder then, if in his partial eyes
That simple dress a monarch's robe ontvies:
What wonder if far prouder it is worn
Than all the fashions that the town adorn?

XXVI.

My country grey! so sober, neat and warm,
Ne'er may our youth despise thy simple charm,

Nor scorn to don thy modest plain array,
For all the gaudy tissues of the gay;
Still be the comfort of our clime, and long
As years of freedom in our annals throng,
Thy garb of sweet simplicity maintain
The home-bred virtues of the rural train.

XXVII.

The rosy girls in brighter colours, fair,
And ribbons knotted on their folded hair,
With merry smiles and sparkling glances please,
Contrive new conquests and old lovers tease.
So Eve's fair daughters, on whatever ground,
In polished cities, or in back-woods found,
The courtly beauty, or, the rustic maid,
Alike invoke the graces to their aid;
Alike ambitious, ply each gentle art
To spread the sweet dominion of the heart.

XXVIII.

At length assembled in the spacious room
Where blazing logs disperse the early gloom,
In pairs together drawn, they side by side,
In circle round the hearth, their task divide,
With hearts as busy as their fingers, till
Love's gentle magnet draws each yielding will.
But vain to tell what tales, and glances sly,
What nudges pass and secret whispers fly,
Or half in earnest half in jest the while,
How true-love spells the prying maids beguile,
To count the apple seeds and toss the rind,
To learn the name that Fate for each designed;
While oft in sport the half-resisted kiss
Returned in earnest seals a life of bliss.

XXIX.

Their labour done, they crowd the festive board.

With game and fruit and country dainties stored;
O'er sparkling cups with mead and cider crowned,
The humour broadens and the laugh goes round.
Old Ranger John, with stronger potions blest,
Sits monarch of the feast with song and jest.
His iron cheek relaxes, smiling bright,
His shaggy eye beams with a youth's delight,
As low he stoops and in some maiden's ears
Repeats the flatteries of his younger years.
Then all at once the merry viol sounds,
The tambourine the jolly note rebounds,
And on the springing floor, with sparkling eyes
And tingling feet the ready dancers rise.

XXX.

See, blithe Euretta, young and debonair,
With Eric rises light as summer air;
And rosy Gertrude, love lit in her eye,
With Herman, hand in hand will gaily fly;
And Ethwald too, the witching music warms,
Bright eyes invite and blooming beauty charms
For Isabelle was near and in her smiles,
The imaged sweetness of Constance beguiles.
In double row arranged with mirthful din,
Each foot beats time impatient to begin,
When Ranger John with buxom blushing Nance
Throws off his years and leads the smiling dance.
Now all in motion music wings their feet;
Moist fingers join, and glances glances meet;
The tender pressure of the circling arm
At every turn adds fire to bosoms warm;
Life kindles love and as they bound along,
One pulse of harmony beats through the joyous throng.

XXXI.

Extatic joy! behold each willing pair,

The pleasing task and equal burthen share;
And now advancing, now retiring, show
How life and love's commingling currents flow.
The youth approaching the coquettish fair,
Sees her retire with well-dissembled air;
To other youths resign her fickle hand,
Change round the dance and smile on all the band.
As he in turn withdraws, the maid relents
With smiles allures him back, and he repents;
Till hand in hand, the mazy circle run,
The pair unite and end as they begun.
A picture this of the inconstant maid,
Vain of her charms; for conquest all arrayed;
From heart to heart she roves through every sign
Of love's bright zodiac, with power divine,
Though dear the youth late captured by her wiles,
Still dearer he just tangled in her smiles,
The last still best beloved, till he in turn
To grace her triumph will rejected mourn.

XXXII.

Thus every figure to a thinking mind
Shows something more than simple mirth designed,
And Gravity might sit with pondering glance,
Extracting morals from the shifting dance.
O blissful hours! when sports like these can please!
And lightsome hearts enjoy their native ease;
When scorned the pampered revels of the great
Our rural youth maintain their simple state.
Blest like their sires with vigorous health, and fraught
With feelings uncorrupt and generous thought,
Their souls attuned to music's gay refrains
No envious gloom their native mirth restrains;
Out all disburthened own th' attractive power,
And old and young enjoy life's fleeting hour!

Canto Seventh

I.

Thus pass the Autumn days; The fields are shorn;
From floor to roof the barns are filled with corn;
The glorious apples dropping ripe to see,
Wait the last shaking of the burthened tree;
Each oak with acorns and each bush with seed
For beasts and birds is stored 'gainst winter's need.
Then Boreas opens wide his icy door,
And clouds and fogs and tempests issuing pour;
The foul East winds with sweeping pinions fly
And driving sleet conceals both earth and sky,
Till dark December comes with frosty brow,
And all our Northern land is wrapt in snow.

II.

Season of gaiety! that far and near
The forest land unites in social cheer.
When tinkling bells vibrate the frosty air,
And glittering snows the flying sledges bear,
The youths and maids, in pliant furs enrolled,
Crowd in defiant of the biting cold,
While eyes meet eyes that fired with mirth and love,
Shine doubly radiant like the stars above,
Hearts draw to hearts and blithsome laugh and song,
The pleasures of the winter ride prolong.
Be praised ye wintry hours! when keen and bright
The stars shine nearer, and the Northern light
Gleams like the Halls of Odin, when the train
Of flashing spears march forth to Valhal's plain,
Where day by day the heroes join in fight,
And on the mead-floor revel every night
With Asgard's Gods, until that final morn,
When from creation's verge sounds Heimdal's horn
That Time's no more; and born of Hel's dark womb,

7

Twilight of horror shades the day of doom,
Yggdrasil shakes and moans in every bough,
And Surtur's flaming sword lays all creation low.

III.

But Spring at length breathes life into the woods
And willows first unfold their tender buds;
The leafing maple glows with ruddy hues,
Pale green the ash and budding beech, endues;
The dogwood flowering ere its leaves appear
With snow white blossom crowns the early year,
The grass peeps verdant from the melting snow
And springs and brooks brimful careering go,
While in the sunshine bright all creatures move
In earth and air, with joyful notes of love.
But vernal gales long hoped for, came at last;
And like eolian breathings o'er him passed;
As with his father's blessings on his head
Across th' Atlantic waters, Ethwald sped,
And saw once more above the stormy sea,
The chalky cliffs of Albion, rising free,
Upon whose base the surging billows roar,
Th' eternal guardians of Britannia's shore.

IV.

All hail! he cried, my country's stormy strand!
Ne'er fall the trident from thy royal hand,
Sea-throned Britain! Nor thy flag be furled!
Freedom's last guardian in a slaved world!
Mother of men! by mighty deeds confessed,
And God-ordained to guide and school the rest;
Accept the filial homage, thy just part,
From me and mine and each Canadian heart!
What though thy bounds too strait to hold the flood,
Of boiling energies that fret thy blood,
With overflowing thoughts that seek for room,

In earth's extremities ; 'tis Nature's doom
That all the tribes of man shall see the face
And own the sceptre of thy mighty race.
The wondering nations of the world shall call
Thee great, and just, and good above them all.
Thy boundless empire linked in one vast state
Shall stand the arbitress of human fate,
And lasping time grow old beneath thy sway
But yet half-reached its full meridian day !

V.

Fondly he kissed the dear desired shore
With love as deep as son to mother bore ;
Ever admiring as he passed along
The charms of England and the scenes of song !
The hills with verdure crowned; the fruitful plains,
Secluded villages and shady lanes.
Now mansions peering 'mid surrounding trees
Where cawing rooks float on the evening breeze;
Now cots half-hid behind the trellised rose
'Neath spreading elms and fields where flocks repose
By placid streams, where fair reflected down
From craggy heights, old feudal castles frown;
Telling of ancient times, that stirred the blood
When England's barons by the charter stood;
Or later days of Freedom's stormy youth,
When all, alike in loyalty and truth,
With honest purpose, girt the warrior's steel
For KING or CAUSE ; but all for England's weal.

VI.

'Mid-Nature's scenes so beautiful and fair,
The crown of all, the free-born man was there,
Brown-haired and blooming with the lineal vein
Of martial Hengist's Anglo-Saxon train;
Or sea-king's progeny that later passed,

With raven-banner floating on their mast,
From isle and fiord of Scania's rocky shore,
To build their homes in England ever-more.
A mighty race, free as the winds that blow,
Who tread the earth and rule where'er they go;
Who bear the torch of Science, clear and bright,
And plant the seeds of freedom, and of right;
Teaching the runes of God, and gracious plan,
Of our redemption, to the tribes of man.

VII.

But Ethwald hasting on the wings of love,
And buoyant as the homeward carrier dove
Nor stayed nor loitered till he reached the dale,
And trod the margin of the winding Swale;
His native stream, whose silvery pebbles shone
With gladness; and whose old melodious tone
Hailed him returned, as down the grassy bank,
He ran as when a boy and stooped and drank,
And ran and drank again, and dashed the stream
Till years of absence seemed a morning dream.
His heart beat wildly as he neared the grove
That witnessed his last parting vows of love;
Those still enduring oaks of ancient days,
That heard the bearded Druids' mystic lays,
Now like a Mother's mantle softly wound
About her son, their shadow folds him round.

VIII.

Within that calm retreat, upon a stone
Sat gentle Constance, musing all alone
With thoughts beyond the seas, while half her ear
Inclined to list the stock-doves cooing near,
And warbling linnets on the hazel sprays
That filled the air with sweet-piped merry lays.
Ah me! she said, in vain I hear you sing;

Your lovesome notes but sad remembrance bring;
For thus you sang in happy days of yore,
Ere Fate called Ethwald from his native shore;
Ere I was left to start at every breeze
That told of distant lands and stormy seas.
Sweet birds, my heart is sick; no more you charm
As when I rested on his faithful arm,
And in these flowery wood-paths loitered long
And joined your liquid melody of song.

IX.

Thus Constance murmured.   Lovlier Nymph than she
Ne'er joined the fairy dance 'neath green-wood tree ;
To woman grown, her perfect form betrayed
The matchless graces that her soul arrayed;
Her auburn locks shade thick her modest brow
And veil the dimples in her cheek of snow,
Where hope too long delayed had blanched the rose
And pensive looks revealed the heart's soft woes.
With sudden flight, aloft in aerial rings,
Two snow-white doves arose on fluttering wings,
And silent fell the grove, as 'neath the shade
Quick falling footsteps neared the startled maid.

X.

Attentive half she rose with lips apart,
A flashing thought shot through her beating heart ;
She knew the sound! love's instinct in her ear
Forebodes these steps her long lost Ethwald bear.
Now red, now white, the trembling maiden turned
As hope and fear alternate chilled and burned ;
Expectance reached its agonizing flood,
When lo ! his form divides the underwood !
She saw, she knew, and to his bosom sprung
His arms enfold her while speech failed his tongue;
Ethwald ! Ethwald ! she cried, tis truly thou !

And rapturous kissed him as he bended low ;
With faintness sinking in her joy's alarms
She still convulsive pressed him in her arms ;
Till bursting tears at last her vision freed,
She looked again and saw twas he indeed.
A long kind look of love, at once he knew
Her heart still his, as ever frank and true,
With silent joy he held her in his arms,
Fondly caressed and viewed her glowing charms,
Till their first transport over, side by side
They poured in words their souls' long pent-up tide.

XI.

With heart-felt gladness 'neath her father's roof,
Ethwald was welcomed and received the proof,
And pledge of favour dearer than his life,
Which gave him Constance, his betrothed, to wife.
Soon down the dale the happy tidings ran
That Ethwald was returned, a brave young man ;
And old and young congratulating came
To show the love they bore his honoured name.
The bridal-day arrived and on the morn
Fresh garlands and green bays the house adorn ;
As antique custom ordered, which prevails
Th' unwritten law of these secluded dales.
Then to the ancient Church, of kin and friends
A lengthened train the happy pair attends,
With wedding favours flying rich and gay,
While chimed the merry bells the live-long day.
The ponderous doors deep-set in arches strong,
Unfolded to admit the joyous throng.
The holy calm within the lofty choir,
Filled all with awe, and quenched each vain desire.

XII.

An ancient house it was and dear to all

Was every stone upon its storied wall.
Old sculptured names upon the paved floor
Told of their ancestors in days of yore,
Who in that place had worshipped ages long
With holy litanies and Sabbath song.
The high-arched aisles were filled with mellow light
Through painted windows glorious to the sight,
That showed on dusky tombs with age decayed
Crusading knights and sculptured matrons laid.
Upon the fretted roof high over head,
Th' admiring swains their martial story read :
Old banners hung and dark emblazoned shields
Their fearless fathers bore from bloody fields ;
From Standard Day and Flodden's broken spears ;
From Cressy's glorious plain and Poictiers,
Where Swaledale's arrows flew like drifting snow,
And France transpierced fell 'neath the long yew bow ;
While Fame's eternal trumpets still recall
The free-born yeoman victor over all.

XIII.

Before the altar, ranged on either hand
Six blooming maids, the bride's companions stand,
Who Yorkist roses in white chaplets wore,
And sprigs of rosemary and pansies bore.
The sprightly youths in happy groups around,
Admire the bride and lightly tread the ground ;
While robed in white the aged Pastor stands
Receives the pair and joins their willing hands,
And blessed their vows, and prayed to God above
With choicest gifts to crown their faithful love.
When home returned, before the joyous band,
So custom bade, the bride and bridegroom stand
Ere they repass the door, and scatter round
The mystic cake in fragments on the ground.

XIV.

An ancient rite that from their fathers came

When heathen offerings were devoid of blame,
And Freya, from her roomy halls above
Propitious smiled upon the vows of love.
With sport and feasting then the day declined;
Fleet-footed youths long-breathed as the wind,
In emulous race o'er many a furlong bound,
To win the flowing garter's silken round.
Then blithe at eve, the pipes and viels play,
And merry dancers foot the night away,
Till they behold the cheek of rising Morn
Glow like the blushes that the bride adorn.

XV.

O, happy pair! and love, thus richly crowned
With nuptial garlands and the zone unbound.
Thrice happy pair! who reap the due reward
Of youthful vows, and long preserved regard.
Conjugial love! to innocence decreed,
Of virgin hearts alone, the golden meed!
The sacred emblem that doth type and show
The great Creator's love for man below.
The lord of life himself, nor deems it shame
To bear the bridegroom's honorable name;
And with the pure in heart consummate too,
The mystic marriage of the Good and True.

XVI.

The Good and True! behold the secret mine
Of nuptial happiness and life divine!
The golden chain, draws nature to its goal,
And joins the sweet espousals of the soul.
See why *the Pair*, in wisdom was designed
For mutual help to form one perfect mind;
One finished arch, where love and reason bright,
Man's truth and woman's tenderness unite,
With hues diviner than the gorgeous bow

That seals God's covenant with earth below.
In gentle woman's soft and beauteous mien,
The great Creator's tender love is seen;
On harsher man is drawn the squarer line
And graver lineaments of truth divine.

XVII.

Such was their Union in his primal plan,
When male and female, God created man,
And the great Archetype as he designed,
Stamped his own image upon human-kind;
When Truth and Love drew each to each, alone,
And man stood up, though twain—a perfect one.
Thus virtue only forms the lasting band
Perpetuates the union of the hand,
When youth decays and early passions chill,
Preserves the pristine admiration still,
And as the aged pair approach the tomb,
Decks it with garlands and dispels its gloom.
The golden chain of true connubial love
Joins earth with heaven and both with God above,
Its links electric with his Grace o'erflow
And bind forever, all they bound below.

XVIII.

Eanwald returned, and in the Forest-land
Was welcomed back by many a eager hand.
Greeting his bride, they one and all declare
The truest heart had won the fairest fair.
But none more joyful than his father sped,
And o'er his threshold, Constance fondly led.
As once the shadow on the dial ring
Turned backward for a sign to Judah's king,
So Walwyn's heart rejoicing with his boy
Renewed its youth and warmed with former joy.
She, like a household deity adored.

His hearth's domestic charm again restored;
Her lightsome presence shed a genial ray
As warm and bright as beams of rosy May.
His happy roof now seemed a vernal sky
Where auras breathe and birds of heaven fly;
A canopy of loveliness which crowned
Some blest parterre of Eden's hallowed ground;
Where every thought fresh opening like a flower
Fragrant with sweetest odours decked a bower,
Which to enjoy, Kings might their state disdain
And Saints look down and sigh for earth again.

XIX.

Thus passed their days and each successive morn
Saw peace and happiness their house adorn;
Their social hearth with wisdom's converse fraught
By all the wise and good was widely sought.
Old Ranger John who daily came to greet
There held his place and spread his buskined feet,
Oft wiled the winter hours with tales and strains
Of the first settlers on Canadian plains;
Their toils, their hardships, and his proudest theme,
Their loyalty that shed its flashing beam
Through war's dark clouds until resplendant, grand
Its cloudless sun rose on the Forest land.
With themes like these he filled the listening youth,
With love of country and with loyal truth;
Till as he fanned the patriotic flame
They glowed to emulate their father's fame.

Canto Eighth.

I.

Thus time passed on. The leaves again turn sear
And wailing winds lament the dying year,

The dry grass rustles, and as Autumn cools
The crisping ice creeps o'er the shallow pools,
The pleasant birds are gone, and through the day,
The lonely grey-bird chirps and screams the jay;
The sullen woods their golden visions past,
Throw back to heaven the frowns upon them cast.
One dark December eve, thick clouds arose
Their darksome folds pregnant with speedy snows;
The stars gazed dimly and in gusty floods
The wind swept round and wailed amid the woods,
Shrill barked the fox and oft the ghostly owl,
Shrieked to the watch-dog's long complaining howl,
While deeply boomed the hoarse incessant roar
Of angry waves that lashed Ontario's shore.

II.

Old Walwyn's household round the blazing hearth
Heard the winds whistle with defiant mirth.
As sank the night outside, in deeper gloom;
Within, more cheerful glowed the lighted room.
The moments winged with pleasantness embrace
The fleeting hours, and pass with nimble pace;
And the sweet lull of happiness at home
Like holy incense fills the peaceful dome.
Fast by the warm and blazing ingle-side
The father sat in patriarchal pride,
And poured his pleasant thoughts with genial glee
Like golden sunset on a summer's sea.
Stretched at his feet a shaggy sheep-dog rolled
An ancient keeper of his master's fold,
Now invalided from his fleecy care
He lies the guardian of his easy chair.

III.

Near by sat Constance, loving and beloved
And at her knee a cradle gently moved,

Where sleeping lay a little cherub face,
On which she fondly gazed and sought to trace
With all a mother's pride and wife's desire
The imaged features of its manly Sire.
Ethwald who guessed her thoughts looked on and
        smiled,
For he saw but the mother in the child,
Deemed that alone her looks and mien it bore
And for the fancy loved it all the more.
In other rooms apart, young Eric's tongue
With glee unmeasured, like a viel rung
Amid his comrades who his labours shared;
Snow-shoes and guns they vigorously prepared;
Elate that rugged Winter brought again
The stirring pastimes of the rural train,
The keen pursuit, the rifle's deadly crack,
The barbecue and forest bivouac.

IV.

One winter night like this, the ban-dogs' bark
Warned of some step approaching, in the dark,
And Eric hastened out to calm the din
Of angry dogs and lead the stranger in.
He soon returned conducting by the hand,
All drenched with water and befouled with sand,
A hapless fugitive of negro birth,
Who craved a corner of their kindly hearth,
And begged with timid voice and drooping head
Their roof's protection and a crust of bread.

V.

His yellow skin betrayed the mingled vein
That brands the white man with eternal shame,
The hideous truth revealing to the sun
That Africa's revenge at last is won;
That Europe's blood polluted as the grave,

Quails 'neath the lash and trembles in the stave ;
By Nature's outraged laws condemned to live
And bear the yoke and chain it wont to give,
Groaning in more than African despair
Where slave and master common kindred share.
The marks of early age, his features bore,
And stamp of bondage in their aspect wore,
His eyes subdued looked stealthily around
And 'neath the white-man's gaze sank to the ground ;
Yet showed at times, were liberty to win
That an elastic soul coiled up within.
Deformed by early toil appeared his frame
And clothed in rags that covered but in name.
His naked feet were swollen, travel-torn,
Bruised with stones and pierced with many a thorn,
And oozing out afresh where'er he stood
Left every footstep marked with his blood.

VI.

Ere half his wants were named, old Walwyn came,
And placed him by the hearth's reviving flame,
While melted with compassion, Constance ran,
Brought food and raiment to the wretched man,
Plucked out the thorns that pierced his bleeding feet
And dressed his wounds with ointment cool and sweet,
And spake with kind encouragement to cheer
His humble spirit's timid abject fear,
For born beneath the yoke and bred a slave
His soul lay buried in a living grave,
Brow-beat and humbled by the white-man's scorn
And shrinking as the snail's uncovered horn,
Such courtesy unwonted, now to find,
Among the race of tyrants o'er his kind,
With wonder glued his tongue, and in amaze
His grateful eyes looked up with silent praise.

VII.

Soon o'er the glad expression of his face

A sudden cloud eclipsed each sunny trace,
Upon his swarthy palms he sunk his head
And in a tone of anguish feebly said :
My children, O, my children ! can it be
Your hapless Sire rejoices to be free ;
Eats the sweet bread of kindness as he hears
The music tone of freedom in his ears
While you, O weary woe ! 'mong whips and chains
Naked and hungry, toil on Texan plains ?

VIII.

Unhappy man ! said Walwyn, com'st thou then,
To find a refuge from that Southern den,
Where weak to all but thy devoted race
The laws to license yield the foremost place ;
And Freedom once a Goddess chaste and proud·
Is turned a harlot midst the wanton crowd ?
Comest thou from that new land, shame of the earth,
The hag of slavery's last accursed birth,
Where like a flood long fretful of its bounds
Bondage has overflowed the virgin grounds ?

IX.

Kind master, no ! the fugitive responds :
In Tennessee I wore the accursed bonds ;
My native land, if but the Negro dare
Reclaim a portion in its balmy air.
Ah ! soft its clime and rich its sunny glades
Clear roll its streams, and cool its forest shades,
Where climbs the clustering vine, and pendant down
The luscious paw-paw droops its purple crown.
There sweet at eve the mock-bird's mimic song
Deludes the groves as with a feathered throng,
Of merry warblers emulous of fame,
Chanting by turns to win the foremost name.

X.

Such is my native country, rich and fair,
A land I love despite my soul's despair;
Despair for half her sons in servile chains,
And ranked with the beasts that graze the plains.
Yet, crowning all their wretchedness beside,
Their very claim to manhood's self, denied,
And the eternal soul their Maker gave;
Declared to perish in the Negro's grave!
My thrice unhappy race! how long, how long,
Must they yet writhe beneath th' oppressor's thong,
And summoned at the dawn of morning grey
In famished herds out-toil the summer-day?
Will never rise that holy Christian morn
When mute shall lie the shrill plantation horn;
When Freemen blithe, no more of labour coy,
Unwarned will seek the field with songs of joy?

XI.

O, thankless masters! cannot ages long
Of true obedience plead the negro's wrong;
Shamed by the meekness of his patient race
Unbind his bonds and soothe his long disgrace?
His unambitious heart would still desire
To serve you, happy with a freeman's hire,
To you all higher cares would freely give
Content in humble usefulness to live;
Or must his servitude to your commands
The manacles lock faster on his hands,
Till his despair burst forth in mighty words
And forge his fetters into gleaming swords
On every hill give freedom's summons breath,
And boldly strike for liberty or death?

XII.

Half rising as he spoke, the Negro's eye

Glared red as lightning in the midnight sky,
His voice rose wild, and fierce, his swarthy hand
Grasped empty space for an avenging brand?
But soon the moment's frenzy like a tide
In rapid ebb, fell from its fancied pride,
And down amid the quicksands of his grief
His spirit sank, a wreck beyond relief.
Constance, her eye-lids tremulous with tears,
His children's fate still ringing in her ears;
For woman's tender feelings cannot rest ·
When cught crosses her maternal breast,
The care of things to man she will forego,
Where frigid reason rules the bosom's glow,
But one domestic sorrow moves her frame
With instant sympathy and pity's melting flame.

XIII.

She asked of his partner's mournful fate,
And of their children's thrice unhappy state;
Each from the other torn, a helpless prey,
To other climes in bondage sold away.
Ah, gentle lady! mournfully he spake;
Why should our sorrows make your bosom ache,
And scarce my feeble lips with power avail
To coin my breath to such a piteous tale?
Ah! who can tell when all are rent apart
The desolation of a parent's heart;
When every point the changing breezes blow
Wafts in his ears their parting shrieks of woe.

XIV.

Sad was her fate, companion of my life
Thrice hapless mother and despairing wife!
Forced from my arms and dragged to regions strange.
Where slavery's self is cursed by the change,
To Georgian swamps, where pestilential death

Makes thick the air and poisons every breath;
Where every morn more fearful seems to rise,
Save that which opens on her dying eyes.
And my poor little ones! woe, woe the hour!
That they were born beneath the tyrant's power;
Perhaps, dread thought! and yet with justice rife,
To curse their parents for the gift of life.

XV.

Well might she tremble on yon fatal day
She saw the trader mark his future prey;
The greedy fiend survey her little brood
And in his soul revolve the price of blood.
And as beneath the hen the chickens fly
To seek concealment from the falcon's eye;
So with instinctive fear my children flew
To her the only refuge that they knew.
But frail defence! not feebler is the wing
To shield its chickens from the falcon's spring,
Than the slave mother's agonizing prayer
To save her offspring from the trader's snare.

XVI.

The Trader! yes! the wretch whose guilty hand,
Black with pollution ransacks all the land,
Buys man for money and with avarice cold,
Exchanges human wretchedness for gold!
All manacled and chained from place to place,
He drives our harmless unresisting race,
And in the market sees with stony heart
Sire, wife and child forever torn apart,
Sold far away to many a Southern shore
To toil in slavery till life's no more.

XVII.

O, heartless monsters! O, enduring grief!
Of all your cruelties, this is the chief!

8

His very bonds seemed lighter, while you gave
Domestic refuge to the hapless slave.
And while one chain encircled each and all
He bowed his head and lived your passive thrall.
That time the trader passed, but short our joys
His wolfish eyes had marked our darling boys,
His greedy avarice counted all the gains
Their little limbs would bring on Texan plains,
On Texan plains where all the South had run,
To quench the brightness of the Aztec sun;
Tore up the tree of Freedom planted there
And sowed the weeds of slavery and despair.

XVIII.

But fleet our hopes of respite, short our bliss!
That very day he called my children his,
His! yes, his slaves, his beasts, his chattels, all
Robbed of their soul and body, each his thrall
To toil till death beneath a slave's vile name
For stripes and hunger, nakedness and shame.
But as the plunderer leaves the callow nest
Until the fledgelings raise their feathered crest;
So he, but to betray with surer cast,
Spared for a time to seize on all at last.

XIX.

The day arrived which saw the human hound
Of blood returning on his homeward round,
His markets made, with herds of wretched slaves
In proud Virginia bought for Southern graves,
The trader came again, and fore my face,
At one fell swoop seized all my helpless race.
I ran and kneeled at my master's feet,
To beg for mercy, and his soul intreat
That he would save them, or at least bestow
On me the welcome curse of common woe.

But vain I plead; the monster cast me off
With cruel blows and cold contemptuous scoff;
And bade his drivers scourge me to my task
Nor let me dare again approach to ask..

XX.

With frenzied eye I saw my children bound
Their necks in couples like the collared hound,
Their little hands affixed to a chain
And dumb with terror driven o'er the plain.
And their poor mother, no! my feeble tongue
Can find no utterance for the grief that rung,
Within our hut, when she of hope bereft
Fell on my neck and learned that none was left,
And clapped her hands and shrieked the live-long night
Till morning mocking with its hateful light,
Again drove us to toil, till night allow
Th' unseen indulgence of forbidden woe.

XXI.

Nor ended here my thrice accursed fate.
Still blacker woes stood waiting at the gate;
And from the cup, a Fiend would shame to fill
We drank the bitterest lees of human ill.
Another trader came; he bought my wife
The sole remaining solace of my life,
To Georgian rice swamps, she was sent apart
From me forever, striken to the heart,
With none to love and solace, or to spread
Their hands to heaven above her dying head.
O Power above! hast thou no bolt of fire
Thrice heated in the furnace of thy ire,
That red and glowing with divinest hate
Will blast such misdeeds, like the stroke of fate?
O'erwhelmed with grief, I fled; and in the shades

Of Cypress-swamps and gloomy ever-glades,
Where alligator foul and slimy snake
Share the dominion of the poisonous brake,
Sought refuge, safer in the panther's den,
Than in the cruel haunts of tyrant men.

XXII.

There long I wandered; oft I pondering stood,
And conned and conned the added debt of blood,
Till turned my brain, with maddening fancies rife,
And slid my hand instinctive to my knife;
And something whispered terrible and clear
Dread words of vengeance in my ringing ear:
Mango return! And in the thicket hide
Wherein thy master takes his evening ride;
Amid the aldar bushes wait thy foe,
And take thy vengeance with a single blow.
I turned me round, but living thing saw none,
Except a serpent coiled on a stone,
Its brilliant eyes flashed with unearthly fire,
That seemed to tempt me to my fell desire.

XXIII.

I turned my steps and ere the gorgeous sun
Dipt in the Western wilds, my goal was won;
And on a rock I whet with savage mood
The knife that glittered for my tyrant's blood.
With ear upon the ground, intent I lay,
And listened keen, and chid his long delay,
Till lo! a hoof-beat jars the sighing breeze,
A figure glances 'neath the shady trees;
'Tis he! but what, but what, un-nerves my hand?
Be firm my soul, let vengeance bear command
O'er every sinew! But what trembling here
Shoots through my heart as he draws swiftly near?
"Thou shalt not murder! Tis thy brother's blood!"

Methought a voice rang through the darkening wood.
I thought of what was oft in whispers spread;
His sire was mine in sin and shame ; twas said
That my bond-mother, helpless in her fall,
Bore me a father's slave, a brother's thrall.
I gazed on his face, and spared his life,
My hand relaxed and dropped the glittering knife,
And I stood fixed in horror, doubtful, mute,
Till he was passed and safe from my pursuit.

XXIV.

The dire temptation left me, and I lay
Weak as an infant, till with parted day,
The heavy dews fell on me. I arose
And lighter felt the burthen of my woes.
My hand was clean ; the blood I sought, unspilt,
And 'mid my sorrows I was free from guilt.
But where to flee ? I cried ; for ne'er again
The driver's scourge shall lash me o'er the plain.
Amid these wilds, I cannot, dare not stay
Where blood-hounds chase to death their human prey.
O, whither shall I flee ? I groaned aloud—
When Night stood mantled in her starry shroud,
And with her finger pointing to the North,
Showed me the star of Freedom beaming forth;
The lamp of hope, whose fixed and constant ray
Lights the dark path that leads to life and day.

XXV.

Oft in the silent night, was whispered round
The weary groups of slaves stretched on the ground,
That in the distant North, the polar star
Shines o'er a land that Slavery doth not mar ;
Where equal laws and equal freedom, fall
Like dews of heaven, alike refreshing all.
But hard the way and long, with forests, streams,

And mighty lakes to cross; and howls and screams
Of blood-hounds following, and viler men,
And Law with eagle's claws, to seize again
The hapless fugitive from servile chains,
Who dares seek freedom on Canadian plains.
But vain the forests, rivers, lakes and laws
Accursed of God; in vain their eagle's claws,
In vain the blood-hound's fangs and viler men
In hot pursuit, to seize or slay us, when
The foot unfettered springs from servile chains,
To seek sweet freedom on Canadian plains.

XXVI.

With soul revived, I fled towards the ray
That shone before and cheered the dubious way,
Until the curly clouds of breaking morn
Bade me conceal till night again return.
Thus weary weeks I passed; a man forbid;
By night I travelled and by day I hid;
I gleaned the fields of scattered ears of corn,
And ate the berries of the tangled thorn;
My drink the forest spring, my bed the rocks,
Shared with the hissing snake and lurking fox;
Till wearied out at last, I saw with tears
The stream that flows along your bold frontiers.
Upon my face the winds of freedom blew,
And deep, deep draughts of liberty I drew,
As o'er the brimming river's misty haze,
The land of refuge met my longing gaze.

XXVII.

With throbbing heart from out the woods I hied,
With boughs and drift-wood to the water side,
And framed a raft of sticks and faggots, bound
With supple vines well knotted round and round.
Last night I durst not launch; for where I lay,

I saw, I heard, My God! forgive I pray!
Why told I not before?   Say know you not
The secret Councils held in yonder spot?
All looked amazed; and Walwyn wondering said,
What Councils, man?   Why break thy story's thread
With this abruptness?   We are nought allied
To the cabals that vex the other side.
Ah, Sir! cried Mango, tis not as you think;
Danger's afoot! and pendent o'er the brink
Of ruin hangs your land, while many a foe
Prepares to plunge her in the gulf below!

XXVIII.

Last night in Tonawanda's woods I lay,
And heard them counsel till the break of day;
A band of armed men, whose chief I knew,
Known in the South, as Desperado Hugh.
A dark conspiracy they had in hand,
Combined with traitors in your slumbering land.
And from their speech, I gathered 'twas their aim,
Soon as burst forth Rebellion's sudden flame,
Amid the wild confusion, like a flood
To sweep your shores with rapine, fire and blood.
This very night, again their Council sits
At midnight hour, as best such deed befits;
The place, Grand Island; and if nothing bar
Their purpose then is to begin the war.

Canto Ninth.

I.

All looked in wonder at so strange a tale,
And half belief or total doubt prevail;
When Ethwald questioning, rapidly replies:

Man ! speakest thou truth or art inventing lies ?
Rebellion ! War ! Thou talkest dreams I ween,
Or thy confused thoughts mistake the scene.
We hear the French below, are ill at rest,
With crooked counsels and vain hopes possessed ;
But War ! Rebellion in the Upper Land !
And armed invasion lurking close at hand !
It cannot be ! for few I trow would change
Their native laws for others, new and strange.
Though many may and many will debate
And strive for dominance within the state ;
Yet who so mad as speak a traitor's word,
Or raise a traitor's hand or crave a foreign sword ?

II.

While Ethwald spake incredulous ; behold !
A distant shout upon the night breeze rolled.
All list intent, and for a moment's space
Regard each other with inquiring face.
Father of peace ! said Walwyn, hast thou then
Withdrawn thy spirit from those factious men ;
And must the bitter seed of angry words
Grow to a harvest of unsheathed swords ?
Forbid kind heaven, for all their sakes ! but hear
Those deep-voiced shouts increasing still more near !
What can it mean ? said Ethwald : Sir ! they shew
The negro's tidings are alas ! too true.
Horsemen approach ! I hear their clattering feet ;
Your rifles, boys ! and we will forth to meet
Whoever comes ; and compassing their fate,
Will learn their errand at the outer gate,

III.

They sallied out, and saw with watchful heed
A troop of fiery riders come with speed:
The rising moon gave out a pallid light,

Which showed them armed.   Far echoing through the
      night,
First Ethwald hailed ; but ere he well begun,
Answered the mighty voice of Ranger John,
Who on a fiery steed led on the train,
Keen as a wild Pawnee that scours the Western plain.
Ethwald ! he cried, and grasped his hand full fast,
" All doubts are ended, and 'tis fight, at last !
Rebellion rises, and bold Head's commands
Have left the issue to our loyal hands !"

IV.

By this, the troop of horsemen filled the green
And well-known voices shout : God save the Queen !
Grey-headed sires and manly sons were there,
And boys scarce able yet their arms to bear ;
Guns in their hands and bayonets by their side,
With scarlet ribbons in bold favours tied.
Clad in their rural garb as chance decreed
Each man had sprung upon his fleetest steed,
While many a female figure drew the rein,
Or sat behind some brave and loyal swain ;
Sister or wife, who came helpful in need,
Home from the lines to guide his gallant steed.

V.

The lovely daughters of the Forest land !
Who left your hearths at loyalty's command,
And with your presence sanctified the cause
That armed your brothers to defend the laws !
Be his false harp for ever-more unstrung ;
And torpid silence poured upon his tongue ;
In Fame's great book unwritten be his lays
Who would not join the anthem of your praise.
Blest women ! from whose lips our children claim
The bright traditions of their father's fame ;

Beneath whose lessons their young hearts expand
With loyalty to king and native land.
Thrice blest our Country ! when its mothers true
Give the just precept and example too ;
And from the cradle to the grave inspire,
The noble virtues that the patriot fire.

VI.

Old John whom eighty years had not depressed,
Stood like a towering hemlock 'mid the rest,
Which scathed with age and tempests, still doth grow
Green and luxuriant to its topmost bough.
A crimson sash in ample folds arrayed,
The colours of the royal cause displayed;
And clad in simple grey, no arms he wore,
Save one bright tomahawk his girdle bore.
With martial voice he halted all the band,
Few were his words, and mild his quick command,
As turned he hastily in Walwyn's door
To tell his news and con their bearing o'er.

VII.

Walwyn ! said he, the hour is now at hand.
Toronto's bells boom o'er the startled land.
Despairing Faction thwarted of its sway
Gathers its strength and forms its last array,
Lifts war's red banner and rebellious runs
Unto th' arbitrement of pikes and guns.
He touched the glittering hatchet by his side,
And sternly smiled, and said: It has been tried ;
Through two hot wars faithful it served the King
Flashing in vengeance like the lightning's wing ;
Behold the shaft, all notched from heel to head;
Each notch the token of a traitor dead !
Though old my hand, my grasp is firm and keen
Again to lift it for my youthful Queen.

VIII.

A score of years is off my shoulders cast
Since spurring messengers this night have passed
With summons to proud Lincoln's loyal train
To meet at day-break on Niagara plain.
Ere falls the dust raised by the courier's steed,
The country rises at this hour of need,
To guard the lines, and send a chosen band
To save Toronto from the Rebel's hand.
Rejoice my friend, at last the loyal sword
Will cut the coil of treason, thrice abhorred,
And with sharp logic of convincing steel
End the disputes that shake the common-weal.

IX.

Old Walwyn grasped the Ranger's hand and said:
We will go with thee John, however sped;
Myself and sons though new to war and strife
Shrink not from duty for the sake of life.
Yet, let me counsel mercy ; for I feel
Tis with a sort of joy thou drawst the steel
Upon thy brethren, whom to lawless deeds
The sad delusion of the moment leads.
Dupes more than traitors, call them—Few I ween
In heart are rebels to their gentle Queen.
Weak in their numbers; but far weaker still
In their resolve to work enduring ill;
Misled, deceived, by the guilty few,
Whose vile ambition cheats the simple crew;
They riot run, nor guess the moving cause
That drives them to oppose their country's laws.

X.

I cannot truly think they mean to stand
Rebellious to their Queen and native land;

For midst their errors they revere the fame
And love the glories of the British name.
Have mercy then! and as thou strikest, extend
One hand in peace and bid the quarrel end:
For hear me John!—I tell thee Walwyn; No!
By God above! withhold I not one blow!
Thus answered he, while anger and surprize
Flushed on his cheek and fired his frowning eyes.

XI.

Thou plead for rebels! thou! But that I know
Thy heart is loyal though thy hand be slow,
Here on thy hearth I'd brand thee with their shame,
And put the blotch of treason on thy name,
"Our brethren," callest thou them? tis false I ween,
Aliens they, both to our land and Queen !
The spawn of them who cast our people forth
To perish in the deserts of the north !
Who burnt our homes, our nearest, dearest slew
With tortures that would melt the Devil's crew,
Crawl in our goodly land and study o'er
The traitorous lessons they have learnt before.

XII.

Walwyn, thou art too kind, and mercy's part
Misguides thy reason and deludes thy heart.
Thou hast not seen as I, the fatal truth,
How boldness waxes with untimely ruth ;
And gentleness brings ruin, when the hand
Of armed revolt is lifted in the land.
Dupes though they be, this, this, is not the time,
To plead for peace and palliate their crime,
Ere we have crushed their hopes and broke the spell
Whose strong delusion leads them to rebel.

XIII.

No, Walwyn, no! I swear by God above ;

My Sovereign's honour and by all I love,
This hand unarmed with their's shall never meet
Till insurrection crouches at our feet.
They seek sharp arguments, and with full hand
We'll deal the logic which they understand!
They call the storm; and on their bloody path
Will raise the whirlwind of the people's wrath.
For lo! through all the land with bounding feet,
Our loyal bands flock to the armed leet,
To fence with hedge of steel their sovereign's cause,
Their country's honour and their native laws.
But winnowed in the roaring blast of war,
When yon seditious chaff is blown afar;
When on the earth this foul rebellion lies,
Plucked by the roots, trampt down, and withered dies,
Let blue-eyed Mercy on the wretched men,
Unveil her face, and smile sweet pardon then.

XIV.

Old Walwyn half-reproachfully replied:
Thou judgest harshly, John! it were my pride
As tis my duty, equal with thine own,
To save my country and defend the crown;
To venture all I have, both land and life,
For sake of peace to end this cruel strife.
Albeit, I share not in thy gladness; no!
My heart is heavy at the coming woe:
The shame of treason in a land like ours;
The bitter rage that tramples freedom's flowers
In gory mire, while quakes the land with fears,
With orphans' wailing filled, and widows' tears.

XV.

Moreover John, this night are tidings come
Will make us all rise up for hearth and home:
This weary man from slavery hither run,

Crossed o'er the lines this eve at setting sun.
Last night in Touawanda's woods he lay
And saw a council sit till break of day;
The delegates and leaders of a den
Of desperadoes, thieves and broken men,
Who wait the signal of rebellion's roar
To pour their bands on our defenceless shore.
To-night the plot unravels, and they meet
Where long Grand Isle divides the waters fleet,
To take their last resolves, and hurry in,
To share the spoils the rebels hope to win.

XVI.

Struck with the news, the armed men press near,
Lean on their guns, and lend attentive ear;
Their eyes flashed fire, but none the silence broke
Till Ranger John with calm decision spoke
'Tis as I thought! that vile rebellious band
Plot with the stranger to subvert the land,
Their wretched faction else would never dare
Unfurl a traitor's flag in British air.
He called the fugitive, and questioned keen
Of all that he had heard or guessed or seen;
Then musing stood, and for a moment eyed
The gallant youths that clustered by his side.
We are too few; he said, for deed so bold
Or we would seize them in their secret hold,
And lack the means to cross the rapid stream
Ere they disperse, or early morning beam.

XVII.

Ethwald, my friend—the night is wearing late
Our country trembles in the scale of Fate,
Saddle thy swiftest steed and ride with me
For my own eyes would yonder council see.
They will not cross to-night, and I would know

The strength and bearing of this plotting foe.
And Herman, my brave son, go thou along,
Thy heart is steady and thy hand is strong ;
And take your rifles, good in case of need
For there is danger in the daring deed.
And Walwyn thou and thine will all attend
Our brave companions to their journey's end :
And we will join you at the rendezvous
With certain tidings of the midnight crew.
My darling Constance ! cried he, why these fears ?
Thy Ethwald will return ; nay, spare thy tears,
That look of thine might melt the hardest heart
That ever threw or met death's mortal dart.

XVIII.

She scarcely heard, for with unwonted fears,
For Ethwald had she only eyes and ears ;
While paler than the lilly of the flood
And cold as marble by his side she stood.
Ethwald ! said she, thou knowest that cruel dream
That once I dreamed by our native stream.
With strange distinctness and prophetic power,
It gazes on me at this fearful hour !
What can it mean ? O mercy, blind my eyes !
Nor let such cruel fantasies arise.
Avert the omen ; which my gloomy fear,
Interprets to thy death approaching near.

XIX.

Hark ! Herman's voice ; who calls thee forth to go,
And share his danger mid yon secret foe ;
Nor may my arms withhold, nor lips implore,
That thou shouldst shrink to meet the battle's roar.
I can not, no ! thyself would first despise
My coward fears and unprevailing eyes ;
For well I know thy heart is raised above

All earthly wishes in thy country's love;
And while I weep the dangers of the fray
I would not breathe a wish for thee away.
Ah, would to heaven, 1 might on thee attend
Thy faithful wife, companion and friend.
For though I could not lift the fatal gun
And terror-struck would see the blood drops run;
Yet I might stand a buckler by thy side,
With my true bosom thee from harm divide;
Receive the deadly stroke for thee decreed,
And for my Ethwald saved, exulting bleed.

XX.

Sweet Constance! answered he; thy words inspire,
And feed with holy oil, the patriot fire:
Approving eyes like thine, though wet with tears,
Purge worthy souls of misty doubts and fears;
In every nerve the sap of manhood pour,
And make us true to duty, all endure.
Droop not dear wife! nor brood on yonder dream;
Nor this, nor that, th' interpretation deem;
Since God alone, who rules the when and how
Of mortal fate, what's best will not forego,
And but reveals at times his hidden plan,
For special ends to unbelieving man.

XXI.

Then with a smile where sadness seemed to shade
The native sweetness which his face arrayed,
He silent stood, as if intent to hear
Some secret whisper in his inward ear.
Wrapt for a moment in a waking dream,
With light supernal all his features gleam.
He took her hand and gazing on their child,
Which slept unconscious 'mid the tumult wild.
He stooped and kissed its dimpled rosy cheek,

Constance, he said, when he shall learn to speak,
Be truth forever native to his tongue,
And virtue's chosen ways to him belong,
Instruct him day by day, and year by year,
His king to honour and his God to fear ;
For virtue's noblest school is ever found
Where truth and loyalty do most abound.

XXII.

With deep emotion trembling, she replied :
His father's bright example be his guide,
But if stern Fate forbid his father's care
Who else the sacred charge shall fitly bear ?
No, Ethwald, no, alas ! it cannot be !
How shall I teach him if bereft of thee ?
When thou my soul's true councillor, no more
Wilt prompt my lips with wisdom's precious lore ?
Yet, as the forest tree exalts the vine,
May thy example lift his soul to thine ;
Clasp his young tendrils as they reach above,
And bind them fast to heaven with cords of love.
My Ethwald ! well I know, thy eyes sedate
Prophetic see the coming stroke of fate ;
Through thy fond smiles I look, and clearly there
I read a doom that fills me with despair.

XXIII.

Constance ! he said, O; why from thee conceal
The sure presentiment I inly feel,
I feel but fear not.. Yes ! my darling wife,
This coming war demands thy Ethwald's life !
Let not thy heart lament with too much grief,
Turn to a gracious God and find relief,
Recall his promises and trust his power
To give thee comfort in that trying hour.
Live for our infant's sake, his truest guide,

9

To teach him how his father lived and died;
His little feet the ways of vice to shun,
And on the hills of truth exulting run;
While every virtue in his soul shall be
Perfect the more, more he resembles thee.

XXIV.

Adieu! she cried, I hear them call thy name,
To join the ranks of loyalty and fame.
Let this fond kiss, the last perhaps we share.
My heart's undying sympathy declare;
On thy dear lips remain with power divine
And life or death, seal me forever thine.
Yet stay, upon thy breast this token seen;
The badge of fealty to our youthful Queen;
While with thee goes my heart to meet her foes.
Will show I gave thee to defend her cause.
Upon his breast a scarlet knot she tied,
Gave one embrace and parted from his side,
Knelt by her boy and wept, while he with speed
Sprang with his rifle on his pawing steed.

XXV.

Loud as a trumpet then, cried Ranger John:—
To horse! militia! and with speed ride on!
Nor be the laggards of the gallant swains
Who join their colours on Niagara plains.
All mount in haste, impatient of delay,
Reform their column on the dark highway,
Bid their old Captain speed, and as they bound
The clattering hoofs dint deep the frozen ground.
Old John, a moment stood, intent to hear,
As burst their distant shout upon his ear,
Said he : That's Eric's voice! I know it well,
I taught him when a lad, the Indian yell;
His buoyant heart now dances wild with joy

And throbs for battle; brave and noble boy!
Come Herman now to horse! to horse! he cried
The night wears on, and we have far to ride;
Grasp firm your bridles and with careful heed
Press through the forest paths where I will lead.

XXVI.

He spake, and bounding o'er the dusky plain
And closely followed by the eager twain,
Soon struck the woods, nor once their speed allayed
But headlong galloped 'neath the forest shade,
Where showers of withered leaves rose as they passed,
As if uplifted by the whirlwind's blast.
The frowning trees that hemmed their narrow way,
Contrary-wise flew by in dense array;
And frosty glades and brooks that half congeal
Are whirled behind the courser's flying heel.
Thus on they sped, as when the demon horn
Rings through Germania's woods from night to morn,
And the Wild Yager spurs his spectre steed,
And all th' infernal hunt pass with unholy speed.

XXVII.

Thus rushing on, at length before their eyes,
They saw the dark one-sided mountain rise,
Whose rocky shoulder lifts and firm sustains
The vast expansion of the upper plains.
Upon its rugged slope dense forests hung,
And hoary rocks above the forests sprung,
That wreathed again with trees their stony brow
And coldly eyed the level plains below.
Swift came the horsemen, and in front descried
The deep ravine that breached the mountain's side,
Where hanging woods and jutting rocks invade
The gloomy pass that winds beneath their shade.

XXVIII.

The crescent moon just tipped the lofty trees
That fringed the sky and shivered in the breeze,
While blackest night 'neath Dian's silver bow
Crouched in the glen and refuge found below.
Still rushing on, th' impetuous coursers came,
With smoking nostrils and with heels of flame,
As up the stony road with wild rebound
The iron hoofs beat fast the hollow ground.
Soon they surmount and clear the close ravine,
The lofty banks withdraw their rugged screen,
And sweeping to the South as on they ride
The upper plains spread out in prospect wide.

XXIX.

The riders halted on the lofty height
And backwards looking through the silver night,
They breathe their steeds, and from the mountain's
          brow
Survey the glorious landscape spread below.
A sea of forests that for ages grew;
And belts of open, where the axe passed through:
With fields and farmsteads veiled in night's soft pall,
And church and mill that rise distinct from all.
Still further on; a streak 'tween earth and sky,
The dark deep waters of Ontario lie:
Their distant roar borne on the laden breeze;
Joins the deep murmur of the host of trees,
Whose sturdy boughs have shed their leaves in showers
And stripped to wrestle with grim Winter's powers.

XXX.

Ethwald, towards the scene stretched out his hand,
And cried; who would not fight for such a land?
Who would not die, ere tongue of man should say

The Forest land became the foeman's prey ?
Its soil be hallowed, unto all who know
The happy homes that yonder lie below;
The homes where honest Virtue native lives,
Where Hospitality profusely gives,
And simple manners closer greet the heart
Than all the gilded compliments of art.
Accursed be he that draws a traitor's knife
In land like this, and kindles civil strife!
Thrice cursed the deed, by God and man abhorred,
To cross its threshold with a foreign sword!

XXXI.

And that shall never be! young Herman said:
No traitor shall uncrown Victoria's head!
Nor from her diadem one jewel steal,
Nor tramp Canadian plains with hostile heel!
Ethwald, my comrade dear! my joy and pride
Were to defend my country by thy side,
Nor grudge my duty, nor deny my life,
To share with thee, the coming day of strife.
Thou knowest this hand that once in Sherbrook wood,
Choked the grim panther 'mid her tawny brood.
Thou knowest my rifle; it is very sure;
Thou knowest my heart; as yonder rock secure;
By thy right hand I'll stay, and in the tide
And rush of battle fight we side by side.

XXXII.

Ethwald compressed his hand and warmly spoke:
Thou worthy scion of a mighty oak;
In calm of peace or storm of iron fight
On thee will never fall dishonour's blight;
I take thy loyal hand,.and by thy side
Will gladly share whatever Fate betide.
Yet, Herman, by a token sure, I feel

My thread of life fast running off the reel,
And would not thou partook the fatal blow,
Ere long will sever me from all below.
Yet go I forth with gladness ; though I hear
The tread of Death behind me, striding near ;
He will not grasp my hand ere honor's won,
My country saved and my duty done.

Canto Tenth.

I.

As they conversed apart, old John stood high
Upon a rock that loomed against the sky,
And searched with piercing gaze the ocean grey
Of woods and waters that beneath him lay—
Then sudden wheeled his horse and to them came,
Said he : my eyes have seen the proof of shame.
Upon Toronto's heights a fiery star
Glares on th' horizon like the eye of war,
And through the startled land with bloody glow
Proclaims the gathering of the rebel foe.
He spake, and o'er the lines with rapid flight,
A rocket rose, and vanished from the sight ;
Like many a brilliant hope that mounts the skies
And in its fancied heaven fades and dies.

II.

The old man spread his hands and cried elate ;
I take the omen! such shall be their fate!
So rise they up, and sink, in night's dark womb,
Our country's curses heaped upon their tomb.
And now my faithful boys ; haste onward ; lo !
You signal marks the rising of the foe,

Push to its utmost stretch each gallant steed,
For life and death are pending on their speed.
They pressed their smoking flanks and forth again
Sprang through the open glades with loosened rein ;
While sharp and shrill the night winds in each ear
Sang a wild cadence to their swift career.

III.

Now passed the haunted grove, where dark and dread
The phantom Chieftain nightly lifts his head,
Stalks round his sunken grave, and in his hand
Lifts up the broken wampum of his band.
Now passed the tall Beech Woods, that sternly keep
Their silent watch where Death's pale captives sleep,
And the red fox hath dug his fulsome den
Amid the dust and bones of armed men.
Kentucky long lamenting, rued the day
She sent her hunters forth in war array ;
Where other woodsmen keener than her own
Tore from her brow her boasted sylvan crown.

IV.

A Chief and Captain then, brave Ranger John
Laid his dark ambush and allured them on
With feigned retreat, till turning, breath to breath,
The foe was compassed in the jaws of death.
From every covert glared the glittering eyes
Of watchful Iroquois, and burst the cries
Of Lincoln's bold Militia, rushing in
To grapple with them and the fight begin.
Loud beat their drums the signal of retreat ;
Fear froze their hearts and winged their flying feet ;
But lo ! no backward path was more to find ;
Death stood before ; Fitz Gibbon pressed behind ;
The friend of Brock, and nobler title none

Ere bore a soldier 'neath our Western sun.
The rifle balls ring sharply as they fly,
And wild platoons of musketry reply;
But vain defence! The invaders sunk at last
Or cowered in heaps beneath the iron blast,
Till in despair they gave their captive hands
To grace the triumph of the rustic bands.

V.

Old John with kindling eye, looked sternly round,
As he rode o'er the well-remembered ground;
A grim relaxing smile broke o'er his face
As loud he muttered:—'Twas a glorious chase!
Gods! how the ambush rose to trap the game,
And from Kentucky cropped her plume of fame!
And showed the Long Knives, spite their forest lore,
A point of woodcraft they ne'er saw before!
Above the graves he leaped his fiery steed,
And through the glades pressed with increased speed;
And struck the broad high-way, where pouring down
From all the uplands to the distant town,
Horsemen and waggons filled with armed men
The road-way throng far as the eye can ken.

VI.

Oft as they hailed him, loud the Ranger's tongue
God save the Queen! the loyal watchword rung,
Which caught from mouth to mouth by all the train
God save the Queen! was thundered back again.
John drew not rein, but rode with lofty crest;
And close behind, his young companions pressed,
Who with their rifles on their shoulders, lay
Bent on their saddles, and devoured the way.
In haste they traversed thus the spacious road
Through fair champains expanded all abroad,
Where undulating fields spread left and right.

All silver frosted in the lunar light.
'Mid orchards, groves and gardens, far and near,
Still homesteads peep and lofty barns appear,
And clustering ricks, and ample sheds that house
The shivering flocks in Winter's bitter snows.

VII.

But passed the riders on till Lundy's Lane
Crossed the round hill that tops the glorious plain,
Whose thirsty sands once drank the reeking gore
Of dense battalions from Columbia's shore,
Who vainly rushed where England's cannon crowned
The flaming summit of the guarded mound.
O glorious spot! The true Canadian's pride,
How oft thy story thrills the ingle-side;
When some old warrior shows his honest scars
Refights his battles and renews his wars!
Such brave old Secord! didst thou use to stand
The admiration of our youthful band,
Who keen to hear of battle's martial roar
Hung on thy lips and thirsted still for more,
While thy true eloquence, our bosoms gave
To feel the thrill that animates the brave.

VIII.

Or round McDougal crowded, when he told
Of meeting armies and of drums that rolled.
Oft as the fortunes of the foe prevail
With burning cheeks was heard his thickening tale;
Elate with pride! as turned the stubborn fight,
When flashing guns illumed the pitchy night,
When volleying lines of stern Militia stood
'Neath England's banners on the field of blood,
And side by side with her red-coated sons
Pressed to the charge and laboured at the guns.
When the long columns of assailing foes

With rapid step the fiery summit rose;
While storms of grape-shot rent their serried band,
And flashing bayonets met them hand in hand;
Then few to many, Lincoln all defied;
And fierce Glengarry's wrath ploughed deep and wide;
And Erin's vengeful yell came wild and shrill,
With English cheers that thundered down the hill,
Unequal to the shock, the foes recoil,
Their starry banners trampled in the soil;
To Freedom's sword their broken legions yield
The victor's laurels and the death-strown field.

IX.

As Ranger John rode past, he pointing said;
On yonder dusky spot, we burned the dead.
Too many to inter, the gathered slain
Were piled in heaps and burnt upon the plain.
The great, the small, the brave, the base, the proud,
All wrapt together in one fiery shroud,
With mingled ashes undistinguished lay
Shrunk up to handfuls, at the close of day!
High blazed the funeral pyres, and endless rolled
Black clouds of smoke revolving fold on fold
Across the waste frontiers, and sadly bore
Their gibbering ghosts back to their native shore.
Such was the end of that invading host
Our Country's conquest made their haughty boast;
Such be the fate of every hostile band
That lifts war's banner in the Forest Land!

X.

Now sailed the cloudless moon through seas of light
And dimmed the sleepless stars that watch the night;
As swiftly turning from the sandy lane
The riders crossed a spacious rolling plain,

Hedged by the lofty screen of dusky woods
That hide Niagara's deep-embedded floods.
White clouds of mist rolled upward on the breeze
Swept o'er the brink and dripped among the trees;
While earth and air, in tremour all around,
Shook in dread cadence to the rumbling sound
That rises up from Nature's troubled womb,
With roar unbroken till the day of doom.
They hurried on; the woody veil withdrew,
The wondrous vision swept full into view;
Niagara's twin-horn Cataracts descend
And eye and ear with their contention rend.
A spot of chaos, from Creation's day,
Left unsubdued to show the world alway,
What was the earth ere God's commandment ran,
That light should be, and order first began.

XI.

The riders halt, and for a moment stay,
While Ranger John half chid the brief delay.
Though often seen before, with fresh desire
The glorious vision still they each admire.
Spread o'er the South, a furious tumbling sea
Rolls down the steep incline, as wild and free
As when with tossing heads and flowing manes,
The desert steeds in herds sweep o'er the plains.
As in th' Olympic Stadium's final round,
The chariot wheels revolve with thundering sound,
While veiled in clouds of dust, the Champions fly
And shouts and turmoil shake the earth and sky:

XII.

Thus down the rocky rapids, side by side
A thousand foaming currents madly ride;
Now mingling, now dividing, each and all
Still swifter hurry to the final goal.

There, waves that washed Superior's rocky strand
And rolled transparent o'er her silver sand,
So pure and limpid that they seemed to bear
The bark canoe afloat in very air,
Now lashed to madness, o'er the rapids ran
Yoked to the darker waves of Michigan ;
St. Clair's shoal streams and Huron's haunted floods
That trembled round the Manitoulin woods,
And fretful Erie's waters, in dismay,
Sweep white with terror down the shelvy way.

XIII.

In vain, Goat Island, dank, and grim with scars,
Of an eternity of watery wars,
With stony shoulder stems the rushing tides
That right and left his dripping shore divides.
They scape his grasp, and o'er the jutting brink,
Sheer down on either hand impetuous sink ;
The vail of waters rending, as they go,
'Mid storms of mist into the gulf below,
Where, face to face, the sundered torrents pour
In rival cataracts, with deafening roar,
Mingle their sprays, and with their mighty war
Shake earth's deep centre with eternal jar.

XIV.

That dread abyss ! what mortal tongue may tell
The seething horrors of its watery hell !
Where pent in craggy walls that gird the deep,
Imprisoned tempests howl, and madly sweep
The tortured floods, drifting from side to side
In furious vortices, that circling ride
Around the deep arena ; or set free
From depths unfathomed, bursts a boiling sea
In showers of mist and spray, that leap and bound
Against the dripping rocks ; while loud resound

'Ten thousand thunders, that as one conspire,
To strike the deepest note of Nature's lyre.

XV.

Stupendous scene! from Table Rock we gaze,
All things forgotten, but that magic maze;
Till in th' illusion of a waking dream,
Clouds, rocks, and waters, all commingled seem
To glide beneath our feet, and in one flow
Creation's wreck sinks in the gulf below.
In that extatic hour, then bend thine ear,
O! Nature's son! and purge thy vision clear,
To see a marvel, but to him revealed
Who reads the mystic runes of flood and field.
Amid the droning thunder's outer din,
Sound tinkling harps and harmonies within,
And on his throne beneath the rainbows seen,
Th' eternal Manitou sits all serene
With robes unfluttered, and with look benign,
In great Niagara's holy inmost shrine;
While countless spirits with expanding wing
Float round his throne and ever upwards spring,
In vapoury robes that waving to and fro,
Seek the bright skies and leave the strife below.

XVI.

In silent wonder from the lofty bank,
As Ethwald gazed and all the vision drank
Into his inmost soul, the startling tongue
Of Ranger John above the waters rung.
For he, stern Captain, with impatient mien
Scarce deigned to look on the stupendous scene;
But on the farther shore, where swampy woods
Dip their low branches in the passing floods,
His eyes were fixed; and seizing Ethwald's arm
Dispelled at once the vision's dreamy charm.

Ethwald! said he, thou seest yon ruddy light
That glimmers on the distant verge of night;
It marks the spot where meet the gathered hordes
Of foreign thieves, who draw their lawless swords
Upon our land, and from that secret den
Prepare to issue 'mong the haunts of men.

XVII.

He spake, and at the word, the horsemen bound
Across the plain, and skirt the stony ground,
Nor once drew rein upon the river shore
Until Grand Island lay outstretched before.
In haste dismounted, on the narrow beach
With rapid search a log canoe they reach,
And launching forth upon the rippling tide
With skillful paddles o'er the waters glide.
In silence reach they thus the woody strand,
Where tangled alders crouch upon the sand,
And brush the waters as they swiftly flow
Towards the smoking cataracts below.

XVIII.

In Indian file they passed, with cautious tread,
Towards the spot where fires gleamed wild and red,
And dusky figures moving to and fro,
Betrayed the presence of the plotting foe.
Led by the light, in silence, on they came
Like skillful hunters closing on their game ;
They reach a clump of cedars, and survey,
All ears and eyes, the scene that fore them lay.
An open forest glade, environed round
With doddered oaks, whose branches touch the ground,
With gloomy elms and knotty pines that throw
A pall of blackness on the earth below.
At either end the glade, huge bonfires burned ;
And in the midst a great assembly turned,

And blazing links, a savage rostrum showed.
Where stood the leaders of the motley crowd.
Long piked shafts the pirate flag displayed
The French tricolour, as their symbol made,
And many a banner waved of stripes and stars,
Or lent or stolen for their lawless wars.

XIX.

A varied crowd they seemed, of all degrees;
The wanton ruffians of a land of ease;
Men ever prompt the felon knife to draw,
Minions of night, and scorners of the law,
Vile fugitives from justice, debt and shame;
World-branded thieves and rogues without a name;
Well-clad and ragged, passing rich and poor;
Those who had nought, and those who wanted more;
While every vice that's known in every clime
There pressed its claim to fill the ranks of crime.
Others again, seemed mere deluded tools
Of crafty demagogues: poor dupes and fools,
Whose vain conceit would regulate the sun,
And teach the times and seasons how to run,
And think they rule, while they are only slaves
To do the work of more designing knaves.

XX.

Such was the herd, and scarce distinguished stood
The heads and leaders of the ruffian brood;
Yet as the oldest wolves the pack exceed,
And in the ranks of vice the vilest lead;
So these base chiefs in every look expressed
The gathered virulence of all the rest.
In arms they stood, and guns and pistols bore
And crooked bowie-knives in girdles wore,
While stars upon their hats and every hue
Of martial frippery, appeared in view.

Above the rest, Ranslaer as general stood
The great Bombastes of the mingled brood,
A pompous knave with little wit to guide
His bold assumption and unmeasured pride.

XXI.

Vain-glorious Chief! could thy Batavian name
Forget the heights of Queenston dear to Fame,
Where rank on rank adown the dizzy steep
Thy father's host was hurled into the deep,
Or on the field surrendered, while the cry
Rose in the ranks of Britain: Live or die;
Remember Brock!? Lo! while that height remains
To tell the story to Canadian swains,
My country will remember ever more
Her day of triumph on Niagara's shore;
With mournful pride will view the hallowed rock
Stained with the precious blood of dying Brock;
The Statesman wise and just, the Warrior brave,
The Ruler of the land he died to save;
Whose glorious deeds will live, and from the tomb
His martial Spirit in the day of gloom,
Will whisper: courage! and make strong the hand
Of each defender of the Forest Land.

XXII.

Around Ranslaer there pressed, a noisy crowd
Of base pretenders, who for place elbowed,
And claimed precedence, while they prating stood
Of Freemen's rights to plunder where they would.
One stood apart, a man of martial mien
With earnest seriousness who viewed the scene,
Whose noble countenance and eyes expressed
A manly spirit and a generous breast.
An Exile he from fair Polonia's plains,
What time his country burst her galling chains,

And fought and fell with everlasting fame
Of deeds heroic, and Muscovite shame.

XXIII.

O, brave Von Shoultz! what madness drove thee on
To band with thieves and make their crimes thy own?
To scourge our peaceful shores with fire and blood,
And rouse the Lion in his bitterest mood?
Alas! we know.   Deceived in freedom's name,
And taught that Britons shared thy country's shame;
Thy base companions drew thee in the snare
Of death and danger which they feared to share.
And when betrayed, false honour's fatal laws,
Still bound thee fast to their defeated cause;
Till Justice seized, and spake the dreadful doom
That sent thee to the scaffold and the tomb.
Yet be it spoken o'er thy hapless dust;
That Britons, sternly faithful to their trust,
Mourned while they struck thee down, and might not
        save
The gallant Pole, the deep repentant brave.

XXIV.

Such was the scene that Ranger John beheld
With keen and steady eye; while anger swelled
His loyal heart, as his unerring ears
Detected all their projects, hopes and fears.
As midnight waned, the leaders of the band
In anxious expectation seemed to stand,
Awaiting tidings of Toronto's fall,
The fiery signal, that should summon all
In one wild deluge of invasive war,
To sink the cross, and lift the Southern star.
At length Ranslaer arose, and long and loud
Harangued the still-increasing, boisterous crowd;
As demagogues have done since days of old,
Forged freedom's mark on brass, and called it gold;

And in the name of liberty and right,
Wrought deeds as black as hell's obscurest night.

XXV.

Thus spake Ranslaer: Hail, citizens and Friends!
This night, the haughty rule of Britain ends!
Columbia's mighty destiny is cast;
And all the continent is ours at last!
Now Freedom's sons, like Ocean waves shall roll
In one o'erwhelming tide from pole to pole!
Repaying ancient scorn with modern hate,
Will shake at last the tower of England's State,
Tear down her flaunting banners, and unband
Her regal fetters from Canadian land.
Then courage, Patriots! for traitor's hire
This night will wrap Toronto's halls in fire.
Rebellion's flag unfurling, rush we in,
The golden prize at last is ours to win!.

XXVI.

See, all exposed lie yonder fertile plains,
With no defenders, save untutored swains;
Tories and Tories' brood whom we will kill,
Possess their spoil and share it at our will.
The sodden fools who in rebellion rise,
Who think for them we pluck this golden prize,
Will ask in vain our sympathizing hand
To give them back th' emancipated land.
They, save a few who with ourselves are one,
Against a faction fight, and not the throne;
Their sole pretence in arms, to mend the flaws
And heal the grievances of partial laws.
But if we give them aid, and aid we will,
Till all is compassed to our utmost fill;
From the foundation to the topmost wall,
When once in power we will subvert them all,.

And to ourselves aunex our glorious gains,
The Forest Land and all that it contains ! -

XXVII.

Tims spake Ranslaer and from the boisterous crowd
Rose yells of approbation long and loud ;
While whispered Ranger John : with boastful knave
Like this we need not fear, all odds to brave !
But hark ! come rapid footsteps ; boys, beware !
Speak not, nor move ; but watch with double care !
Those are the messengers who bring the clew
To all the purpose of the rebel crew.
Quick as the old man spake ; a figure cast
His shadow o'er them as he glided past,
Cleaving the yielding crowd, and in the light
Of flaming torches stood revealed to sight.
Of lofty stature seemed he, lithe and strong.
Bold his address and rough his ready tongue ;
His garments travel-stained and disarrayed,
Bore tokens of a hasty journey made.

XXVIII.

He gave no salutation ; but he broke
At once his tidings like a thunder stroke,
That sometimes crashes in the calm blue sky
Of summer days, when storms are drawing nigh.
But Ranger John, quick as the stranger came,
And on his features gleamed the lambent flame,
Sprang forward with a groan and wildly gazed
With heaving breast, and eyes with horror glazed.
He grasped Horman's arm, and choked as he
Essayed to speak, and shook his failing knee,
While sudden perspiration rushed amain
From every pore, as cold as winter rain.

XXIX.

In agony of grief, at length he spake :
'Tis he ! 'Tis Hugh ! my swelling heart, O, break !

Herman ! 'tis thy false brother ! see him stand
A living traitor to his native land !
The runner for yon horde of ruffians vile,
Whose footsteps would the floors of hell defile.
Woe ! woe ! thy father, that he ever gave
The gift of life to that dishonoured slave,
Who on my head, like ashes, sprinkles shame,
And spots with infamy our loyal name !
But by this hand, by Providence decreed,
Unshorn in strength to do the awful deed,
Another morning's sun shall not arise
On his rebellious head and mocking eyes.
And this bright hatchet, which I bore that day
When Woodworth and his band fell in the fray,
And I avenged his murdered kindred, now,
With sharper justice, shall release the vow.

XXX.

He drew his tomahawk, and rose dilate
Dread as th' avenging deity.   Irate
The hatchet quivered like the lightning's flame
As he advanced to smite with surer aim.
Amazed and thunderstruck the young men stood,
But Ethwald grasped him as he left the wood.
Sir ! Sir ! he cried ; what passion leads you on ?
Spare him ! let Mercy plead ! nor leave undone
Our purpose here, nor in your wrath forsake
Your country for your own misfortune's sake !
Ethwald ! I serve my country ! Let me go !
Unhand, I bid you both ! a single blow
Shall venge the foul dishonour to our name,
And tell how I erased the damning shame !

XXXI.

But Ethwald still clung to him, and besought ;
And long against his sparkling anger fought :

My life ere his! he cried; Remember John!
Yourself pronounced the exile of your son:
In foreign lands, made him a stranger grown,
Forget the duty which he owed his own.
You are his father sir, and haply true,
His fatal error may be traced to you,
Who let him go to graft in Southern climes,
His youthful soul with shoots of all their crimes.
This keen reproach so unexpected brought,
Turned the wild current of his angry thought.
Stung to the quick, the old man drooped his head;
Ethwald! thou speakest very harsh; he said;
And yet, O, God! it may, it may be so,
That I myself have brought this heavy woe
Upon my soul: for when he went away,
I could not pardon him, nor bid him stay;
And seeking to amend, from bad to worse
Made him a traitor and our name a curse.

XXXII.

Broke down beneath the thought, his anger fled,
On Ethwald's shoulder sunk his throbbing head:
And for a moment all his vital frame
Seemed racked to dissolution with his shame.
At length the strong man conquered, and he stood
Composed as marble 'neath the shady wood.
Ethwald, said he, I am, though pale my face,
A Chief adopted of the Mohawk race;
And as a warrior, I would brave the stake
And scorn the fires of death for manhood's sake;
So for my country, this more burning pain
Than fiery torture, I will calm sustain.

XXXIII.

My Herman, faithful boy! In thee I'll find
A balm to soothe my lacerated mind;

We'll pray of God oblivion, and I ween
Forget you renegade has ever been.
No more henceforth for ever, shall he be
A son, a brother, unto me and thee;
An outcast from his kindred, he shall stand
Doomed to the justice of his injured land.
Ethwald, 'twas thou who saved him, and us all;
For doubtless we had shared the traitor's fall.
Take thou my thanks; alas! no more am I
A warrior fit in ambuscade to lie.
I'm calm, my children now, and from this place,
Will view unmoved the Rebel's shameless face;
And list the tidings he may haply bear,
And fill the great design that brought us here.

Canto Eleventh.

I.

Then forth they looked again, and saw the crowd
Like white-caps on the Lake when winds blow loud,
Tossed to and fro; so burst a storm of ire
In angry oaths and execrations dire
But over all was heard the voice of Hugh,
The master spirit of the riot crew,
Who like a furnace blast, with words of might
Heated their passions to the topmost height;
For he brought tidings that their secret scheme
To seize Toronto, melted like a dream,
The golden hour had slipped, and weak delay
Had brushed their hopes like cobwebs all away.
That all the land uprising, near and far
Rang with the voice of loyalty and war;
While every side the scattered rebels fled,
And from the tempest hid their forfeit head.

II.

And why, he roared, are all our hopes thus crossed,
Our schemes aborted and our fortunes lost ;
But that some traitor from our midst hath gone
Revealed our counsels and our cause undone?
Yes! by the pit of darkness! as I say:
A purse of gold hath dragged us into day ;
And for the base reward, the wretched thrall,
With double treason has betrayed us all! .
And Roughwood! thou the man! stand forth! he yelled
With rising voice like doubling thunder swelled,
Stand forth! thou hollow-hearted, sordid slave,
And own thy guilt, while Justice digs thy grave!

III.

Ar Hugh denounced the name, the raging throng
Caught up the word that rang from tongue to tongue,
While yells of vengeance in a thousand breaths,
Devote their victim to a thousand deaths.
Their fiery eyes turned on him, each one like
The angry rattlesnake's about to strike.
While some with brandished knives blood-thirsty ran
And from the midst dragged forth the doomed man.
Of fifty years he seemed, but years which passed
Each one succeeding, viler than the last ;
Of stature short, with low and doggish brow ;
Bull-necked and turtle-bellied, legs that bow
'Neath weight of sins, and eyes of lust and guile,
And sensual lips that curled with many a wile
Of craft and meanness, while each vice found place
To stamp the villain on his frowzy face.

IV. .

Arraigned before th' inexorable crowd,
He fills the air with protestations loud

Of injured innocence, as down he kneels
And God and man assails with loud appeals.
With stern denunciation, Hugh replied
To each assertion, that he basely lied.
And in return brought damning proof at last
Of all the treachery his heart forecast;
Of all the secret practices he wrought,
And base rewards for which his soul was bought.

V.

Struck dumb with terror of impending death,
Cold sweats burst o'er him and he gasped for breath.
For answer he had none, so plain and clear
The proofs of all his treachery appear.
His serpent cunning often tried before,
His ready falseness will avail no more ;
While on the earth he knelt with horror rife,
And owned his guilt and abject begged his life.
But that base crowd, though few among them stood
But for the price had sold their father's blood,
Stirred up to madness at their schemes undone,
Pronounced his fate, to die ere morning sun.
Up rose Ranslaer and spoke the lawless doom,
Condemned the traitor to a speedy tomb :
The double spy who sold our golden cause,
To lead us blindfold in the Lion's jaws;
This be his sentence : Down yon sweeping tide.
Chained in an oarless boat, adrift shall glide
This traitor to our cause, and plunging go
To drown his treachery in the Falls below.

VI.

From all the crowd wild approbation rung,
Triumphant jeers rolled off each mocking tongue,
Which half forgot his fault, amid the flood
Of cruel pleasure in the wretch's blood.

Beneath their feet the panting felon lay
Prone on the earth in horror and dismay.
When burst the fatal doom upon his ears
it seemed to galvanize his very fears.
Despair gave strength, and the deep dread of death
In notes of terror forced his gasping breath.

VII.

You cannot mean it! No! so short the date!
So quick resolved! so horrible the fate!
Unspeak your judgement nor in all the bloom
Of mortal sin, consign me to the tomb!
O! Hugh! Ranslaer! upon my bended knee:
Let what I have been, plead for what I be!
Long I have served you and with oaths of blood,
Spread treason's rank infection where I could.
Long I was faithful; and my zealous hand
Knit up the conspiration through the land.
But gold it tempted me, O! woeful day,
That for the dross I sold my life away!
Ranslaer! 'twas gold! 'tis thine, but show me grace
Or thine, Von Shoultz! there's mercy in thy face!
O! for me intercede, I'll give thee all
My hidden store; I'll live thy bounden thrall,
Thy slave of slaves, if thou wilt stretch thy hand
And save me from this death-denouncing band!

VIII.

Thus shrieked the doomed wretch, while rent the air
Derisive yells, that mocked his fruitless prayer,
And every eye, red with infernal fire,
Glared on the victim with impatient ire.
They seized and dragged him headlong to the shore
Like hungry wolves that lap the recking gore,
Each one more eager than the others still,
To tear the prey, and his gaunt maw to fill.

Old Ranger John and his companions bold,
Pressed by the crowd, forsook their leafy hold,
And filled with indignation at the sight,
Mixed with the crowd unnoted in the night.
When Ranger John resolved with daring plan
To seize and carry off the doomed man.

IX.

They hurried to the shore. The traitor stood,
Touching the boat that quivered in the flood;
As oft the dying with prophetic breath,
Foretell the coming of the feet of death,
With sure event; so he with piercing yell,
Rang o'er the murderous band a funeral knell.
O! thrice accursed thieves! your comrade's blood
Will cry against you from the rolling flood!
As I now go alone; so you in crowds,
'Mid flaming fire, and suffocating clouds;
And bursting decks, and masts that awful glide
With blazing banners down the midnight tide,
Shall take the final leap, and meet me there
In everlasting horror and despair.
Mark me! a mighty hand shall thrust you down,
And in yon cataract forever drown!
In that deep hell of waters, every soul
Tossed to and fro, shall never cease to howl
In his despairing torture—but shall be
A mark for wonder to eternity!

X.

They heard no more; for with an awful din
They dragged him to the boat and thrust him in.
Cast from the beach, adown the rapid tide
The trembling caitiff quick began to glide.
Ethwald and Herman on the margin ran
And cast an oar towards the doomed man;

Who missed the precious aid and saw it float
Just out of reach of his descending boat.
Then as a last resource, brave Ethwald flew
With John and Herman, to their own canoe,
And fore the yelling crowd pushed from the shore,
And with swift paddles in the current bore.

XI.

At once revealed beneath the moonlight sheen,
Their looks unknown; but their bold purpose seen;
Amazement seized the throng, and sudden fear
Struck in their hearts some armed band was near.
But Hugh, who better guessed, rushed from the wood
And wading deep into the plashing flood,
He bade them turn their bark and come to land,
Or death should overtake them from his hand.
An instant passed, and twice, young Herman drew
His fatal rifle, ere he saw 'twas Hugh ;
O'erwhelmed with horror,and struck dumb with shame,
Upon the gunwale drooped his deadly aim ;
But Hugh called out again, and as he spoke
The whistling death-shot from his rifle broke,
And swift as lightning pierced young Herman's head,
And on his father's bosom stretched him dead.
Nor word he spake, nor single moan he sent,
His loyal spirit in a moment went ;
And his warm blood but now with vigour rife,
Gushed from the wound with his devoted life.

XII.

A cry of horror from the father rung ;
He clasped his boy, but grief compressed his tongue.
Unhappy sire ! he saw that life was gone,
And knew a brother's hand the deed had done !
While Ethwald's warm and sympathizing heart
Seemed stricken with the fratricidal dart,

And for a moment, lost in silent woe,
They drifted heedless in their sad canoe.
But roused from their extacy of grief
They saw their danger, and with prompt relief,
While bullets hissed around them, turned away
And sought the British shore without delay;
Compelled to leave to his terrific doom
Their wretched object, drifting to his tomb,
Upon the sweeping current's foaming wave,
Beyond the power of mortal man to save.

XIII.

Far in the distance, like a frightened steed
They saw his boat glide on with gathering speed,
And oft amid the roaring of the stream,
Was heard the wretch's wild unearthly scream.
The oar that Ethwald threw him from the land,
Danced on before and mocked his frequent hand,
Stretched out to grasp it o'er the yielding side,
Where like a thing of life, it seemed to glide.
Then in his frenzied eye, it grew a snare
A serpent hissing at his wild despair,
Till Hope with flashing wings flew fast away
And left him to his madness and dismay.
Now Conscience opens wide her glaring eyes,
And shapes of death around his bark arise,
And onward beckon, while each moment's fears
Repay in horror, crimes that lasted years.

XIV.

Thus Roughwood lay all crouching in his sin,
Death roared without, and terror froze within,
As like a hunted hare he gasped for breath
And felt beforehand all the pangs of death.
His hands, convulsive clenched the senseless wood,
That overleaped the dark ,impetuous flood,

Or vainly stretched towards the distant shore,
To lengthen out his life a minute more.
Swept down the steep incline, he felt at last
The rushing stream with sudden swiftness glassed.
And with a shriek of maniac despair,
He shot impetuous through the yawning air,
While thousand thunders round their victim rave
As he sinks headlong in his stormy grave.

XV.

Meanwhile the mournful bark of Ranger John
Bore swiftly to the shore his lifeless son
Where sympathizing woman's tender care
Washed off the blood and cleansed his clotted hair ;
In snowy linen swathed his body round,
And banded carefully the oozing wound.
With many a pitying sigh and melting tear,
They stretch his manly form upon a bier,
Array his solemn couch and watch in turn
The silent tapers that around him burn.

XVI.

Thus lay young Herman, fair in death to see
Like some fresh branch just gathered from a tree :
The hue of life still lingering on his cheek,
His parted lips looked as about to speak,
And but for Death's lone stillness, he might seem
Like one asleep and in a pleasant dream.
Unto the bier his sorrowing father came,
Kissed his pale forehead and invoked his name,
And choking turned away to find relief
In all the silent agony of grief.

XVII.

Long Ethwald stayed disconsolate by the side

Of his dear murdered friend, and sadly cried:
O! mournful night! and thrice ill-fated hour!
That cropt of Lincoln's youth the pride and flower!
And doomed thee, Herman! with the morning star,
The first to perish in this lawless war.
Cut like a thrifty sapling ere its time;
Ere age had roughed its green and early prime;
Behold thee laid! and bitterer than all,
The victim of a brother's fatal ball.
Alas! what words may ease thy father's heart
Pierced in thy murder by a double dart?
That noble heart already bruised with grief,
With wound like this will bleed beyond relief

XVIII.

And when swift-footed Rumour eager hears
The fatal tidings to thy Emma's ears,
Thy maid, the flower of Thorold's lovely plain,
Soul-bound with thee, in love's electric chain,
Alas! too certain, with her Herman's end
Will death invoked, come like a welcome friend.
Or the cool springs of reason ebbing low
Dry up beneath the fervour of her woe.

XIX.

No more shall we behold his nimble hand
Guide the gay pastimes of his native land;
Strike the swift ball or on the silvery flow:
With skilful paddle dart the light canoe.
No more at eve when merry viols ring,
His nimble foot, of all will lightest spring;
Nor his gay smiling lips with vocal mirth,
Make glad the circle of the social hearth.
Ye summer fields! no more will Herman's eye
Your golden sheaves, as gifts of God descry;
His burnished plough-share that like silver shone,

Will now rust in the furrow sad and lone.
Ye stately stags in Sherbrook's leafy shades,
Now rove securely in your green arcades!
The feet once shod with swiftness like your own,
Lie cold and rigid here as sculptured stone.

XX.

O! Herman! dear companion of my life!
Pledged hand in hand to share this cursed strife,
The task of friendship which I deemed thine
By Fate inscrutable is rendered mine;
And mine the tears, to see thee foremost win
The shadowy portals of the world within.
Ah! not to thee came softly, white-robed Death,
With sandalled feet and gentle whispering breath,
A smiling messenger of peace and love
To summon thee to join the choirs above.
No! borne on dusky wings, with ruthless speed
A darker spirit was by fate decreed,
To smite thee with a fratricidal stroke
As sudden as the bolt that rends the oak.

XXI.

But thou wert ready; for the good and brave
Dread not the shadows that surround the grave,
But through its cloudy portals clear descry,
The path of glory leading to the sky.
Yea! thou wert ready and thy duty done;
In thy full strand the golden thread was spun;
And what thou haply left unfinished here,
Will be made perfect in that higher sphere.
Methinks I see th' angelic ones who wait
Around thy couch, all gentle and sedate,
To watch thy spirit waking to the sight,
And new-born vision of immortal light.

XXII.

This holy, still, and soul-subduing calm,
This fragrant odour of celestial balm,
That fills thy silent chamber with its sphere,
Declares the heavenly Watchers present here.
Angelic ones! who walk unseen of man,
Yet all his acts and secret motives scan,
Suggesting holy thought and honest deed,
Teach me like him to follow where you lead.
Let me, like Herman, run my blameless race;
Like him, unshamed look on you face to face;
And when life's gordian knot your hands unbind,
Still watch and comfort those I leave behind.

XXIII.

While Ethwald thus bewailed his murdered friend
The Outlaws' Councils in dissention end.
Moved by the strange events that marked the night,
Each one distrustful stood in sore afright;
Imputing in his heart to all the rest
The secret falsehood which his own possessed.
Stern Hugh, who saw the cause was nigh undone,
And better judged the perils which they run,
With words of might, rough as the boulder-rock
On which he stood, harangued the startled flock;
And counselled wise delay, and ampler power,
A braver leader and a riper hour.
Ranslaer opposed him: for his jealous soul
Burned hot that Hugh disputed his control;
He drew his sword, and vowed to lead his band
And trample down alone, the Forest Land.
Retorting fierce reproof, Hugh warm replied;
And fool, and braggart, to his face applied,
And bade the outlaws take sufficient heed,
Nor run the hazard of the hasty deed.

XXIV.

For like a man, said he, your cause would thrive,
Who thrusts his hand for honey, in the hive,
Ere fire and smoke expel the stinging throng,
Who guard the treasure of their homes from wrong.
I know that land too well, to hope for more
Than hasty plunder of its fertile shore;
For only dare we spoil the lion's den,
While he is roaring in the distant glen.
Let us abide our time, till Gallic arms
Fill all the Lower plains with wild alarms,
And call the forces from the Upper land
To quench the fires that burst on every hand.
Then, comrades, then, myself will lead you in
With sudden raid, for craft not force must win;
Till from the undefended shores we bear
The hoarded wealth of many a tranquil year.

XXV.

But dazzling dreams of conquest, such as see
Ranslaer's weak eyes, and fools purblind as he;
Discard them all! not all the dogs of war,
From Maine's cold sky to Texas' rising star,
Will ever hound the British lion forth,
From his strong covert in the hardy North.
But let us patient fan this Gallic fire,
And fresh revolts insidiously conspire;
And when the flames burst forth, with wild alarms
We'll carry in our sympathizing arms,
And from the troubled waters of debate,
Fish all the plunder of the falling State.

XXVI.

Thus raged the foul dispute; when rose Ranslaer;
The danger distant, he declared for war.

11

Despising weak delay, if fortune smile,
He vowed to cross the strait to Navy Isle.
There fortressed 'mid the waters, he would stand:
Defiant of Fitz Gibbon and his band ;
The men of Gore, and Lincoln's volunteers,
Who march beneath McNab to the Frontiers.
The fame of conquest spreading far and wide,
Would summon to his aid a sweeping tide
Of bold adventurers, who would hither run
To share the spoils of warfare once begun.
Said he : my pledges of success, behold !
Are iron keys worth more than keys of gold,
Which at my bidding will unlock the doors,
And empty twenty arsenals of their stores !
While Law will slumber, and its Guardians smile
Soft disapproval of our deeds, the while ;
We know their meaning ! and with heart and hand
Will conquer for them all the promised land.

XXVII.

But wild dissention raged among the crowd,
And harsh debate was bandied long and loud ;
Till Hugh and those who favoured him, retired,
And left Ranslaer with future conquests fired,
Who spread his banners to the morning sun,
And Navy Island's narrow circle won,
His first and last exploit, that sunk in shame
And poured derision on his luckless name.
But Hugh with deeper guile, thenceforth began
To knit his schemes of plunder into plan.
Surrounded by the boldest and the worst
Of hardy ruffians, he was still the first,
Controlled their councils, and with crafty skill,
Bent their fierce natures to his iron will.

XXVIII.

The clouds long gathering in the wintry North
On Richelieu's plains with blood and fire burst forth !

The simple peasantry of Gallia's race,
By demagogues vile arts, delusions base,
And passions blinded with imagined wrongs,
Become the dupes of traitors' subtle tongues.
They raise the banner of revolt; and soon
The torch of war turns night to awful noon;
While burning homesteads cast a crimson glow,
And bloody furrows mark the virgin snow.
On every side, poor helpless women fly,
With wailing babes, beneath th' inclement sky;
Their little household treasures on their backs;
A wild Jacquerie raging on their tracks;
While following these, troop wolves; and kites and
    crows
Come with the rising sun, and fleck the snows;
Tearing the prey from drifts, that hide in vain
The frozen bodies of the mangled slain.

XXIX.

Anon, stern Law in martial vesture comes;
On Richelieu's banks beat loud the English drums;
And flashing bayonets eager for the fray
Bear down upon the Rebels' close array.
In vain St. Denis for a time withstood;
St. Charles ran red with retributive blood,
While the Arch-traitor who began the strife,
Fled from his host to save his abject life.
Anon, Ottawa's icy bosom bore
A flying throng, who 'scaped the cannon's roar,
While St. Eustache's blazing altars rang
With shrieks despairing. High above the clang
And shout of battle, rose the piteous wail
Of burning victims; when too late, the veil
Torn from their eyes, showed them their leaders gone,
Their tree cut down, and refuge, rescue, none.
Then Mercy stretched her hand intent, to save,
And noble Colborne sheathed his battle glaive;

A heap of ruins but remained to tell
How Order triumphed, and how Treason fell:
A monument forever of the scars
And cruel fortunes of intestine wars.

Canto Twelfth.

I.

A feverish summer passed, and to and fro,
Ran busy Rumour bearing tales of woe.
The guarded lines, with hollow truce, foreshew
That coming winter will the war renew.
But how, or when, will burst the threatening clouds?
Or who will lead the savage outlaw crowds?
What their designs? and how, upheld their power?
Form themes for wonder each recurring hour.
At length November's storms and flaky snows,
Bring nights of watchfulness and days of blows.
Again the swains of Gallic race rebel,
Relight the torch of civil war in hell,
And goaded on by Furies, trample down
Law, Freedom, Peace and Plenty, all their own.
Again with martial mien and angry eyes,
The ready bands of loyal Saxons rise;
With mighty arm upholding England's cause,
They grasp Rebellion's dragon by the jaws ;
And from Beauharnois to Mississquoi plain,
Drag the red monster, mastered, gored and slain.

II.

While civil war thus scourged the lower plains
And led to mutual death their hapless swains;
The hour propitious seemed for Hugh to claim

And prove his title to a Leader's name.
Through all Columbia's States his summons ran,
To warn the secret lodges, every man,
And bid them gather to secure the prize
That tempting lay before their gloating eyes.
The outlaw hordes at once declared Hugh
Their chosen leader, and in order drew
Their dark battalions marshalled by his hand,
For sudden inroad on the Forest Land.
Then swift debarking with his lawless hordes,
On fair St. Lawrence banks they drew their swords,
And from the plains of Prescott looking down,
Prepared to rush upon the startled town.
Ere day-light broke, swift couriers rode amain,
On foaming steeds, with spur and flying rein,
And East and West, and Northward, post on post,
Bore stirring news of the invading host.

III.

As sped the tidings on, the forest sons
Left axe and plough and seized their deadly guns ;
And every woodland path converging down,
Poured forth defenders for the leaguered town.
With martial mien and lineage drawn afar
From hardy clans renowned in Scottish war,
Glengarry's plaided ranks in order came
To vindicate their loyalty and fame.
Prompt at the call appeared a sturdy band,
The belted hunters of the Northern land,
Who tread the snows, and chase with wild halloo,
The shaggy bear and tramping Cariboo.

IV.

And many a woodman of the piny shades
Of dark Ottawa, left his sylvan glades,
His axe and raft, and bared his nervous arm,

To save his country from impending harm.
And more in number still, the rural swains
And gallant yeomen of the upper plains,
Fair Canada's chief honour and reward,
In peace, her pride; in war, her safest guard.
On every inland road, on lake and stream,
They hastened on, impelled by oar and steam ;
Or trains of waggons thundering afar,
Or foaming horses, bear them to the war.

V.

Among the rest with stern composure seen,
And port erect, yet sadness in his mien,
Came Ranger John, leading a gallant band
Of hardy yeomen from Ontario's strand.
Hendrick and Simcoe, loyal sons and true,
For from his heart was plucked unworthy Hugh,
Stood by their aged sire with love and pride
To serve their Queen and country by his side ;
Telling the old traditions of their race,
The debt of hatred Time cannot efface.
Came Walwyn true of heart and kind of word ;
The hand of Justice held no nobler sword
Than that he drew, which but one speck displayed ;
Where dropped a tear upon the shining blade.
At his right hand, with courage all elate
Came Ethwald smiling at the frown of Fate ;
For though his boding spirit all fore-knew,
His country claimed him and he owned the due.
Young Eric, by his side with ardour pressed,
Life in his step and rapture in his breast ;
And oft impatient chid the brief delay,
Withheld his hands from battle's deadly fray.

VI.

Frustrate their bold surprise on Prescott town,

Von Shoultz and Hugh the vain attempt disown;
But where the river margin higher rose,
They trench a camp and dare their gathered foes.
Soon girded around appear the outlaw throng,
With stony walls and pallisadoes strong;
And on the lofty bank, an ancient mill,
Crowns their defence, and forms their citadel;
While Prescott's level plains reveal afar
The land's defenders gathering to the war.

VII.

Hugh traversed to and fro his guarded hold,
Masked all in smiles as false as they were bold,
For deep misgivings in his bosom tell,
His hour is come and rung his funeral knell.
Yet to his hordes he spake with cheerful tone:
Stand fast and true; the day will be our own!
Adjuring them by all that's dear to life,
To meet the coming onset knife to knife;
And rather fall with weapons in their hand,
Than crowd the scaffolds, of the outraged land.

VIII.

A dense battalion stood, whose fiery eyes
And bronzed features told of tropic skies;
My true companions! you! he cried amain,
Who drew your knives on San Jacinto's plain,
And in one furious onset won the day,
And tore an empire from your foes away!
A thousand perils we together saw,
A thousand times defied the feeble law;
And if the snares of Fate have caught us fast,
Like men together we can die at last.
If Fortune's favours are no longer sure,
We'll bravely bear the ill we cannot cure,
And struggling to the last unconquered breath
Drag all we can into the caves of Death.

IX.

The morning air blows chill, and o'er the grey
Disparting mist, rolls up the orb of day,
From tangling forests extricates his beams
And shakes his locks exulting o'er the streams.
Long gazed the Rebel Chief o'er plain and down,
The guarded river and the distant town,
And searched with piercing eye each varied band
Of bold defenders of the Forest Land.
Said he: our doom is sealed, and death or chains
Alone await us from these loyal swains !

X.

He silent gazed again a moment's space,
While flushes red and hot passed o'er his face
My brothers ! Hendrick ! Simcoe ! and my Sire !
May he not turn on me that eye of fire !
I see not Herman, whom above the rest
In boyhood's years I loved and honored best,
Why comes he not to battle by their side ?
Hath harm befallen him ? though time and tide
Have dried the springs of love within my heart,
For him I still could feel a human smart.
But down ! fell conscience ! let thy serpents twine
Round other breasts, in vain they gnaw in mine !
For what to me, if friends and kindred pour
Their maledictions on my final hour ?
My time is come, and here at last I stand,
An open traitor to my native land,
With scarce a wish beyond the speedy gloom
And hoped annihilation of the tomb.

XI.

In silence while he gazed, a gallant train
Of England's soldiers marched upon the plain,
And at their head Dundas impetuous sprang,

As for th' assault his cheery bugles rang.
Hugh rose erect, his hardihood returned,
The thirst of battle in his bosom burned,
He traced his guarded camp and swiftly sped
From side to side with firm and haughty tread;
His bands caught mettle from his cheerful tone,
And half the day already seemed their own.
With ringing cheers advance the Forest sons
In headlong race, upon the opening guns,
And scale with nimble feet the guarded wall,
Where smoke and flame and steel envellop all.

XII.

With courage worthy of a better cause,
Stern Hugh from post to post incessant goes,
And to the storm of battle bares his breast,
Like some broad shield to shelter all the rest.
Vain his defences; in a fiery mass,
Above the wall the hot assailants pass,
And charge his serried ranks and volleys' blaze,
With levelled weapons and with wild huzzas.
So when the dams of winter overflow
And raging torrents pour their melted snow,
As higher, higher, swims the foaming tide,
The bulwarks yield, the stony piers divide,
A crevasse opens, and with thundering roar
The sudden deluge sweeps the drowning shore.

XIII.

Ethwald and Hendrick in the very van,
With waving hats before the column ran,
And torn with bullets, carried in their hand
The glorious banners of their native land.
Thus sped th' assault, when Hendrick sudden stood,
While o'er his girdle ran a stream of blood;
Ethwald, said he, I'm shot! and in my side

Like burning coals two rifle bullets glide !
Commend me to my sire, and let him know,
That on the breach I died amid the foe,
And to the last upraised my loyal hand,
To vindicate my Queen and native land.

XIV.

Then turning fiercely, on the foe he rushed,
And twice and thrice his bloody sword he pushed,
And in the very vortex of the strife,
Where clashing arms demanded life for life,
To his dear friend he gave his dying hand,
And breathed his last upon the gory sand.
Scarce Hendrick fell, ere Ethwald bounding on,
In voice of thunder cried—The day is won !
One effort more ! and victory's laurel crown,
And all the trenched camp will be our own !

XV.

But as he spake, a shower of bullets came,
Like hissing serpents winged with blasting flame ;
And one, ah ! moulded in prophetic hour,
When frowning Fate usurped the wand of power,
And evil stars breathed down a poisoned breath,
And gazed malignant from the house of death ;
One fatal ball, ordained above the rest,
Traversed his path and pierced his manly breast ;
He stopped, he staggered, and in mortal pain,
Fell headlong bleeding on the trampled plain.
With cry of agony, his father flew,
And from the press his prostrate body drew ;
And faithful Mango helped them quick to bear
The dying Captain to the outer air.
As they passed through the ranks, a murmur ran
Of deepest sorrow for the wounded man,
And many a fiery eye let fall a tear,
As past they hurried with their burthen dear.

XVI.

Care not for me, he said, the battle's won!
My days are over, but my duty done.
They bore and gently laid him 'neath a tree,
His head reposing on his father's knee;
The glaze of death already filmed his eyes,
That vaguely opened to the azure skies.
With tender care they knelt upon the ground,
And fanned his face and searched his mortal wound,
And brought him water from the margin side
Of broad St. Lawrence rolling in his pride.

XVII.

Unto his heart he drew his father's hands:
But few are left of life's fast ebbing sands:
Send to the front, he said, tell Ranger John,
Hendrick is fallen, and the trench is won;
Their barricades are taken, and the fight,
Towards the mill converges on the right.
Tell Eric too, to come; but ere he spoke
His brother's sobs upon his bosom broke.
Mango the message bore, while Ethwald lay,
Gazed on his brother, and began to say:

XVIII.

I love thee Eric! but thy tears distress;
Assuage thy grief and make my sorrow less;
Prove what our Father taught us both to be;
Resigned, with duty done, to God's decree:
For not a leaf is by the tempest blown,
Save by permission of the Lord alone;
Who calleth man to his eternal rest,
Alone when Mercy orders for the best.
Weep not my honoured father, lend thine ear,
My true affection to my partner bear;

Tell her I freely give this flowing blood,
Nor grieve to perish for my country's good;
Content to think my loyal duty done,
Thus ends in honour as it first begun.

XIX.

But she, the partner of my life and love,
My joy on earth! my hope in Heaven above;
What words to find with consolation rife,
To soothe the bosom of my tender wife?
Ah, Constance! warned of my fate in vain,
Love clung to Hope, and doubted all again;
And unresigned to Fate's severe decree
In widowed sorrow thou wilt weep for me!
My darling boy upon whose infant face,
I loved each feature of her charms to trace,
Be he her consolation, and redress
Her hallowed grief, and with his duty bless.

XX.

Teach him, my brother, 'tis my last command,
His duty to his Queen and native land;
Through good and ill report, all times the same,
Immutable in honour as in name.
Farewell my father! now, yon sunny skies
Grow every moment darker to my eyes;
My feeble pulse irregular and slow,
Will soon be still, and end this mortal throe.
Bright world, farewell! before my closing eyes,
Like breaking morn, I see new day-light rise
On mountain-tops! my native hills! he cried;
And murmuring Constance! turned his face and died.

XXI.

As he expired, the Ranger swiftly came,
Begrimed with battle-smoke and scorched with flame,
His long grey locks uncovered, loosely flew,

And fixed as stone, his rigid features grew.
Few words he spake; but taking Walwyn's hand,
His tear drops mingled with the gory sand;
My Walwyn! faithful friend! 'tis hard, said he;
Fate spares the old, but hews the tender tree.
On yonder bank my gallant Hendrick lies;
And in thy arms thy noble Ethwald dies;
Two lives like theirs, alas! we overpay
The bloody tribute to this cursed day!

XXII.

Said Walwyn, be it as by God decreed;
Reason submits, although the heart will bleed;
We signed the sacred bond, and to it stand,
To die if need be for the Forest Land.
True Walwyn, true! the Ranger rose and said;
But vengeance is a debt must too, be paid!
He raised young Eric swiftly to his side,
And drew his tomahawk, already dyed
With crimson stains, said he: assuage thy grief,
There is a balm in vengeance gives relief;
Lament to-morrow; but to-day is due
For bloody doom upon yon felon crew!
Into the fight they rushed, the front they gain,
Where like a lion Eric trod the plain,
Red was his hand and fierce his frequent yell,
At every stroke he gave, a foeman fell.
Ethwald! for thee! for thee! for thee! he said;
As hideous gasping on the earth they bled;
This, for my father's grief, and this, for mine,
And this, dear Constance! this fell stroke, for thine!

XXIII.

Von Shoultz and Hugh still bravely in the van
Held the sharp conflict balanced man to man;
When tidings spread, Dundas was rushing in

Their main defence, to cut off all within.
Now vainly Hugh implored; nay with his hand,
Struck lifeless many of his flying band,
Who turn in panic fear, and wildly crave
That mercy from their foes, they never gave.
There is no refuge more ! base craven hounds !
The voice of Hugh o'er all the tumult sounds,
No choice, save soldiers' deaths upon this plain,
Or Law's grim gibbets for your portion gain !
As thus he spake, a mighty rush came on,
The forest sons led on by Ranger John,
Who like a storm-cloud red with darting fire
Scathe all before them with consuming ire.

XXIV.

Hugh met his father; face to face they stood;
And both recoiled; while rushed the burning blood
In crimson flashes on each brow and cheek,
And for a moment neither dared to speak.
Old John at length in hollow accents said,
As turned his face the pallor of the dead :
Say, art thou Hugh, or is the very light
False witness turned to cheat my troubled sight ?
Speak, hideous vision ! true then can it be
That I behold a rebel here in thee ?
Speak felon ! renegade to all that's good !
Speak murderer stained with thy brother's blood !
Speak earth and heaven ! and me of doubt bereave,
How else, O God ! how else can I believe ?

XXV.

Father ! cried Hugh with wild, imploring cry,
What dreadful mystery do your words imply ?
A rebel, you may call me and may kill,
I own my guilt; deal with me as you will;
But say what mean you by the murderer's name ?

What brother's lost, and how is mine the blame?
Is Herman dead? nay, father look askance!
Nor pierce me through with that terrific glance!

XXVI.

Thou knowest it not; said John; that barbed dart
Then milder rankles in my bleeding heart.
Remember dark Grand Isle, where midnight shared
Your felon councils, and your plans prepared;
And thou with thieves and traitors joined thy hand
To war against thy Queen and native land!
Recall that night's alarm! thy sudden shot!
Thy hand slew Herman on that fatal spot!
And Hendrick fell to-day! O! death divine,
And to be envied ere a life like thine!

XXVII.

A moment mute he stood; while awful grew
The cloud upon his face. His hatchet drew
He slowly, as he spake: Thy father's hand,
Ne'er spared a rebel to his king and land.
Upon my ruined hearthstone where I trod,
Holding thy grandsire's ashes up to God,
I swore the oath of blood, eternal, deep;
That solemn oath thy Father still must keep.
And I were false before the troops of dead,
If I spared one; or turned aside my head
From thee, lost Hugh!—no more! whate'er befall,
The life I gave thee, I must now recall!

XXVIII.

He raised his hand; when his unhappy son,
Threw down his sword, and knelt the ground upon.
Father! he cried; 'tis not to beg my life,
I bow before you and give up the strife!
Forgive me Father! Ere you strike the blow;
Let my submission prove my depth of woe.
My crimes are many, since that hour of ill,

When I left home to riot at my will,
But in my vilest days with madness rife,
I would have given all, for Herman's life.
His blood be on me! only let me plead;
My·hand unwitting in the fatal deed.
Forgive me! and I'll take the stroke of death,
And bless thee, Father! with my latest breath.

XXIX.

Hugh raised his eyes, and for a moment's space,
In silent agony, the father's face
Turned on his son. ;. I cannot! Hugh! he said;
I cannot pardon ere the debt be paid;
Till death shall expiate thy fearful crime,
There's no forgiveness on this side of time.
In this dread moment of suspense, as bright
The father's steel flashed up in heaven's light,
A treacherous shot from Hugh's retreating band,
Stretched their bold leader bleeding on the sand.
Forgive me now! his lips imploring said,
And at his father's feet, his spirit fled.

XXX.

The Ranger started at the sudden stroke;
The mask of iron on his features broke;
And stooping o'er his son, in accents low
Of grief and pity, poured his bitter woe.
My most unhappy boy! thy debt is paid!
By God's compassion hath my arm been stayed.
Now I forgive thee! Justice asks no more,
Upon thy faults be silence ever more,
And let this expiation wipe the shame
Of black dishonour from our loyal name.

XXXI.

Simcoe rushed to the spot; but never knew
The dreadful secret of his brother Hugh;
Nor his assumed name; nor Herman's blood

Shed by his hand upon the midnight flood.
These sorrows, John and Ethwald, as a dread
And untold secret, sacred to the dead,
And shameful to the living, locked within
Thought's darkest cell, where but to look were sin.
Simcoe! the old man said; I still have one
Strong staff in thee, to lean my age upon,
My knees are feeble, and my feet no more
Can bound to battle as in days of yore.
Where Hendrick lies, his every blood-drop drains
A double portion from my aged veins.
Yon flying carrion must not scatheless go;
And thine must be the battle's latest blow.
He leaned on Simcoe's shoulder; boy! he said
This tomahawk I give thee, dyed red
With many a foeman's life; now let me see
My feeble hand restored to strength in thee;
And I'll attend thy steps and count each blow,
Till full our tale of vengeance on the foe.

XXXII.

Brave-Simcoe kissed his father's cheek, and took
The fatal weapon. Thanks my father! look!
In truer hand than mine it never lay,
And I will keep it to my dying day,
Make it my last bequest and on it trace
Th' eternal tokens of our loyal race.
They forward sprang; when cowering from the fight,
The outlaw bands break up in panic flight,
The storm of vengeance follows them, until
They find a present respite in the mill.
But close besieged in the stony den,
Despair and terror press the crowded men;
The white flag waves submission, and at last
The iron hand of justice grips them fast.

XXXIII.

Thus ended Prescott fight, and through the land,

The song of triumph sounded, and the brand
Of lawless war was broken on our shore,
And quenched the felon torch forever more.
Now fell the dew of peace on hill and plain;
The rural bands hung up their arms again;
And all was gladness, save where hearts still bled,
And melting tears fell o'er the honoured dead.

XXXIV.

Walwyn and Ranger John in friendship dear,
Console each other's grief—and year by year.
In summer shade or by the winter's fire,
Hold converse on the themes that never tire:
The tender memories of the fallen brave,
Who gave their lives to vindicate and save,
This loyal heritage of England's own;
This noble land that Britons call their own;
This golden cup of Freedom, void of flaw,
That pours the sacred streams of equal law.
This land of forests, rivers, lakes and plains,
And earnest men, whose proud ambition strains
The leash of Hope, with filial love to stand,
Britannia's worthy sons, adult, at her right hand.

XXXV.

As Time still passes by with noiseless tread,
He wafts a blessing on each silvered head.
Old John sits in his porch, and robins sing
Amid the apple blossoms, while a ring
Of children's children cluster round his knee,
Filled with the spirit of the old U. E.,
Learning to guard, like him, in days of yore
England's proud Empire, One, for ever more.

THE END.

Printed at the "Mail" Office, Niagara. Canada.

ERRATA.